VEGAS HOCKEY, VEGAS STRONG

Written by
Richard Gubbe and Robert Lawson
Design by Richard Gubbe
and Sarah Walters Baird
Copyright © 2023

Dedication

This book is dedicated to all those original "Hockey Pucks" and risk takers who always believed the sport of hockey had a place in Las Vegas. The Gamblers were the pioneers. The outoor game at Caesars was the catalist. The Lowden family then built the ice hockey arena that housed the first Vegas professional hockey team, the Las Vegas Aces, as well as the first youth ice hockey program through USA Hockey. The teams that followed, the Flash, Thunder and Wranglers among them, left an indelible mark in rinks across Vegas, We are grateful for the participation of those who contributed to the book, to those fans who supported their team, and to each team right up and to and including the entire organization of the Vegas Golden Knights NHL Team.

Acknowledgments

We would like to thank the following people for their contributions: Rachel Gubbe (Editor), Peter Gubbe (Editor), Blake Lawson (Cover, Back Cover), Missy Mohr-Lawson, Barb and Bob Edmunds (Editors), Brad Way (Proofreader), Steve Stallworth, Marc Jacobson, Ron Garrett (Las Vegas Entertainment Radio AM 670 KMZQ Las Vegas) Adam Harahuc (Solid State Radion WTGV97.7 FM Lapeer, MI) Sarah Walters Baird (Design Editor), Phil Cooper, Darren Libonati, Martin Kessler, Dan Marrazza, Steve Carp, Ron Kantowski and Bob Shemeligian, Paul and Sue Lowden, Myron Freund and Cal Coleman, Getty Images (Knights photos), Caesars Palace Las Vegas, Los Angeles Kings, USA Hockey, as well as websites Wikipedia, Vegas Golden Knights, NHL.com,, hockeyDB.com, ESPN, CBS Sports, USA Today, and Nice While It Lasted.
Thank you for helping to create and preserve hockey history in Las Vegas.

In Memoria

William (Will) Lowden – (1986 - 2004) One of the first youth hockey players to play organized hockey under Coach Bob Lawson (Co-Author), and to go on to become a USA Hockey Referee, along with winning several championships with his youth hockey teams as a player.

Randy Huartson – Head Scout, Las Vegas Aces and Head Scout, Director of Player Personal, Las Vegas Flash. Randy died of cancer in 2013.

Eric Danielson – Goalie, Las Vegas Aces and Las Vegas Flash.

Special Recognition to Robert Lawson Jr. (deceased), Roberta Lawson (deceased), William (Cobby) Coblentz (deceased).

Table of Contents

Foreword

October 2nd, 2017, the morning after the worst mass shooting in U.S. history stained the Las Vegas Strip, residents began the arduous process of healing, realizing their sanctuary of fun and excitement had been severely damaged.

There was no making sense as to why a shooter from the 32nd floor of Mandalay Bay opened fire on a music festival, killing 60, shooting 413 others, and causing injury to 867 residents and visitors.

In the wake of such a devastating event as the October 1st shootings, the city experienced a rare somber atmosphere. The shockwaves of the shooting rippled through the community and left an indelible mark on the collective consciousness of Las Vegas. The resilience of the city began to shone through, and Las Vegas began a slow process of erasing the horror incurred.

It was quite a remarkable scene to witness skaters gathering in ice facilities to resume their shared passion for skating and the sport of ice hockey, and to prepare for something longtime residents had awaited – an NHL franchise. Their longing was measured in decades when noble attempts to bring hockey had failed. Now, more than ever, they needed something more to ease their pain — a common thread of unity through a sport they loved. The focus shifted to one particular ice rink in Las Vegas, where a special practice session took place. The expansion team named the Vegas Golden Knights was gearing up for its inaugural season, set to begin in just four days with an away game against the Dallas Stars.

In the wake of the recent tragedy in Las Vegas, there was a moment of hesitation about holding an open practice at the Knights' facility. The somber atmosphere surrounding the city made it difficult to proceed with business as usual. However, as the players began to arrive, a shift in perspective occurred.

The beauty of sports lies in the ability to uplift. As the Golden Knights hit the ice for practice, they were determined to prove their worth. They understood the underdog status they carried and were motivated to defy expectations. Their preparations intensified as they worked on their strategies, refined their skills, and built team chemistry, all with the goal of making a strong impression in their inaugural quest.

The players' arrival set the tone for the practice session, and it became immediately apparent that the mood differed from the usual lightheartedness. There was a notable absence of jokes, laughter, or casual banter. It was as if the weight of the recent events had permeated the air, instilling a sense of solemnity among the players.

Hockey flames had flickered in Vegas for nearly 50 years, but only as a fix for transplants who couldn't stay away from the game they loved. Some played semi-pro, and others watched minor league hockey with a dream that someday the NHL would come to grips with the Vegas stigma and yield to Sin City as the gambling capital of the world.

The announcement of the Knights' franchise brought glee, and the date of the home opener was looming. The journey of an expansion team in any professional sport is filled with challenges and uncertainties, but it is also brimming with potential and excitement. The Golden Knights, fueled by the passion and support of their fans, were eager to embark on this new chapter in Las Vegas' sporting history.

The expectations surrounding an expansion team's first season can often be tempered with predictions of challenging times ahead. Many anticipated that the opening game against a well-established team like the Dallas Stars would likely be a difficult one for the Golden Knights. A blowout victory for the experienced team might have been the logical outcome.

After Oct. 1, the Vegas Golden Knights were the elixir Las Vegas needed. The Knights began their inaugural season Oct. 6 and Oct. 7 on the road with victories against Dallas and Phoenix. Vegas had a winner to welcome home with a warm embrace.

Fresh off that 2-0 start, the Golden Knights prepared for a game against Arizona that meant more than any other ever held in the city. The sport of hockey would bring emotionally wounded people together to escape the tragedy that had taken place only a mile away.

The ice was their diversion. It is a testament to the resilience and commitment of athletes who continue to pursue their passions.

The inaugural opening night blazed with the fanfare only Vegas can provide. Then came the moment to recall October 1st. One player articulated the collective sentiment, capturing the somber feeling that had overtaken the crowd when the time came to pay tribute. Deryk Engelland, a local himself, described the event as having a greater purpose beyond playing hockey. At that moment, the fans fully comprehended the significance of Deryk Engelland's words.

He stood with a microphone in one hand and had his glove on in his other hand while holding a hockey stick in the middle of the ice at T-Mobile Arena that Tuesday evening.

The Vegas Golden Knights defenseman would assure you he is considerably more comfortable with the stick, not the microphone. He said he has probably never spoken to more than "20 guys at once." But Las Vegas was his adopted city, and he met his wife, Melissa, here. Engelland delivered a short and powerful speech in an emotional ceremony honoring first responders and victims of the mass shooting.

Jonathan Marchessault lifts the Knight's first Stanley Cup

"Like all of you, I'm proud to call Las Vegas home," Engelland said to an announced crowd of 18,191.

"I met my wife here. Our kids were born here. I know how special this city is. To all the brave first responders who have worked tirelessly and courageously through this whole tragedy, we thank you.

"To the families and friends of the victims, we'll do everything we can to help you and our city heal.

"We are Vegas Strong."

Dropping the first puck in hockey is something special only players and true advocates of the game will ever understand. Excitement and anticipation mixed with anxiety, to name a few.

Once the puck hits the ice, everything else outside that ice rink disappears.

Depending on who is victorious in the battle determines the length of time that game remains within the minds of the participating teams.

The Knights became the first expansion team in NHL history to start 3-0-0 with a 5-2 victory against the Arizona Coyotes. For three hours, The Knights took the minds and thoughts of the fans to another place.
Hockey helped to begin the healing of Las Vegas.

The Golden Knights would go on to become a source of inspiration and unity for Las Vegas, rallying the community in a remarkable way. They would bring relief and resilience to a city in need, exemplifying the power of sports to transcend tragedy and unite people under a common bond. The Vegas Golden Knights came to the rescue.

The Knights were the first Big Four pro sports team in Vegas, but the beginning of the sport came 50 years prior. Although the first endeavors of hockey never lasted, they laid the foundation for the Knights to flourish. The Golden Knights would leave an indelible mark on both; the sport of hockey and the city of Las Vegas just five years later. It would go on to show that sometimes sports can provide more than just entertainment; they can serve as a beacon of strength and a symbol of hope.

The road to Vegas's first Cup and the first title of a Big Four Sports franchise was long and arduous. The road to Vegas's first Cup and the first title of a Big Four Sports was long and arduous. Team names such as the Gamblers, the Aces, the Wranglers, the Flash, and the Thunder are not household names. The Vegas Golden Knights are after winning the Stanley Cup in 2023. The many stories from hockey's past in Las Vegas have never come to light until now. The funny, informative, and never-told-before stories behind the scenes are revealed from the teams that shaped professional hockey in Las Vegas.

Those who were first to take the ice made Vegas Hockey, Vegas Strong.

Chapter 1
Meager Beginnings –
Gamblers and Outlaws

When delving into professional hockey's progression, it is essential to establish a clear distinction between amateur and professional players. In the United States, USA Hockey serves as the primary governing body for hockey players, and their guidelines can provide a framework for defining amateur and professional status.

Typically, the elements distinguishing a player as professional, rather than amateur, are straightforward. The first criterion is that hockey must be the primary source of income for the player. In other words, the player earns a sizable portion of their livelihood through participation in the sport. This could include receiving salary or compensation from a team, endorsements, sponsorships, or other related income streams.

Additionally, a professional player is typically part of a team that is sanctioned by a recognized league. They compete in games and tournaments as part of a full schedule, adhering to the rules and regulations set forth by the governing body. This involvement in organized competition further solidifies their professional status.

By meeting these criteria, a player is considered a professional in the realm of hockey. It is important to note that specific leagues may have their own eligibility requirements and definitions of professional status, so it is essential to consider the guidelines and regulations of the league in question when determining a player's status.

Defining these distinctions is crucial for understanding the dynamics of professional hockey in Vegas, as it allows for clear categorization of players based on their level of involvement and commitment to the sport.

The evolution of ice hockey in the desert led to the NHL granting Las Vegas its first Big Four sports franchise. The sport grew from a few avid players forming a team in the mob-built International Ice Palace to the first-time pro players suited up in Vegas at Caesars Palace, to the triumph of the World Champion Golden Knights.

In 1991, the New York Rangers faced off against the Los Angeles Kings in a heavily promoted and highly anticipated game, marking the first professional hockey event in Las Vegas. The game received significant media coverage and sponsorships, capitalizing on the city's reputation for vibrant entertainment and excitement. The idea of hosting a professional hockey game in the middle of the desert was indeed an unconventional concept.

Rich Rose, the President of Caesars World Sports and an avid hockey fan, conceived the idea in 1988. Initially regarded as a crazy notion, Rose's vision gained momentum when, during a chance phone call, he spoke with Steve Flatow, the NHL's marketing director, and found out that only the team had the decision on where to play the exhibition game.

Although the NHL was sternly against any gambling relationships, every NHL team is allowed to dictate where an exhibition game is played. Unforeseen challenges arose, such as the ice melting the day of the event and a plague of grasshoppers affecting the competition.

Despite these challenges, the game itself represented a significant milestone in the development of professional hockey in Las Vegas. It showcased the city's potential as a hockey market and generated enthusiasm among fans in a budding hockey community.

After reaching an agreement, the selection of the teams was carefully planned. The LA Kings, led by the legendary Wayne Gretzky as team captain, were an obvious choice.

The New York Rangers, Rose's favorite team, were also convinced to participate in the game. Both teams represented some of the best talent in the league and offered a geographical balance, covering the West Coast and East Coast divisions. This landmark event in Seeptember 1991 laid the groundwork for future professional hockey endeavors in Las Vegas.

That was just the beginning of a parade of teams and exhibition games that held anecdotal masterpieces. Humorous and never-told-before exploits of the Flash include the brawl and subsequent expulsion of four-time Stanley Cup champion and member of the 1980 Miracle on Ice gold Medal team, Ken Morrow, in a game with the Vancouver VooDoo. Then there was the contingent of Russian players arrested for shoplifting women's underwear on the Strip and the team practicing outdoors in 100-plus degrees.

The Las Vegas Gamblers in an early team photo.

Key Hockey Dates in Las Vegas before the NHL

- **1968:** The Las Vegas Gamblers begin to play as a senior amateur team. The team played in the International Ice Palace.
- **1970:** The Las Vegas Gamblers begin to play in the Pacific Southwest Hockey League (semi-professional league). They play their last game in Las Vegas in 1971.
- **1971:** Las Vegas Outlaws begin play as an independent professional hockey team. Their first season was one of the best single-season records of any hockey team in Las Vegas history (29-8-4). Their last game is in 1973.
- **1993:** Las Vegas Aces begin play in the semi-pro Pacific Southwest Hockey League. They folded in 1995.
- **1993:** The Las Vegas Thunder (a professional team) begin play in the International Hockey League. Their home rink was the Thomas & Mack Center. They averaged more than 8,000 fans per game.
- **1994:** The Las Vegas Flash begins to play at the Thomas & Mack Center. The Flash roster included NHLPA players currently active on team rosters on NHL teams.
- **1995:** The Las Vegas Ice Dice play in the North America League. They only lasted for one year.
- **1997:** The first Frozen Fury game is played at the MGM Grand. Becomes an annual tradition.
- **1999:** The West Coast Hockey League expands to Las Vegas, and the Las Vegas Junior Aces are introduced.
- **1999:** The Las Vegas Thunder fold. The team had no place to play after UNLV officials refused to negotiate with team owners regarding a new agreement to play at the Thomas & Mack Center.
- **2003:** Las Vegas Wranglers founded as an expansion franchise following ECHL's takeover of the West Coast Hockey League. The team agrees to play at The Orleans.
- **2009:** First NHL Awards banquet held in Las Vegas.
- **2010:** Las Vegas Wranglers become ECHL affiliate for Coyotes.
- **2013:** Wranglers informed lease at Orleans Arena will not be renewed.
- **2014:** Wranglers discuss plans to play at The Plaza in Downtown Las Vegas. Initially, the plan was to play on the roof of a hotel-casino. Then, the potential arena was moved to ground level. Plans to play at The Plaza were canceled in May.
- **2015:** Las Vegas Wranglers officially fold in January 2015. The Wranglers have the highest winning percentage in ECHL history and held 6 ECHL records before it disbanded. They also made two appearances in the Kelly Cup Finals.
- **2017:** The Las Vegas Golden Knights are born.

The Wranglers had Prison Night in prison garb and Pajama Nights when games started at midnight. The Aces were a rag-tag team of thugs, and the team drew packed houses for free beer nights. The Flash, the Aces, and the Wranglers were full of laughs and mishaps.

The public was never privy to the bungles by management, but these stories are now brought to light. The book focuses on each team, each event and every program's contribution, and dives deep into the city's sentiment and long-standing connection to the sport.

The metaphorical phrases like "the desert had indeed frozen over" paint a vivid picture of the juxtaposition of a city known for its desert climate and boxing fame embracing a winter sport.

Much of what transpired in the growth of hockey came from the efforts of authors Bob Lawson and Richard Gubbe. Lawson had brought the Aces into existence and was the architect of the Flash, as well as the creation of youth hockey with his father. Gubbe was the lead coordinator of the game at Caesars and assisted with PR efforts for the Aces, Flash, and youth hockey.

Together, the authors of this book were crucial in forming the triumphant statement, "VEGAS HOCKEY, VEGAS STRONG."

The Pioneers

During the late 1960s and early 1970s, the Las Vegas Gamblers and the Las Vegas Outlaws were notable teams in the area. While their schedules may not have been as extensive as those of professional leagues, their presence and efforts showcased the growing interest and passion for hockey in Las Vegas at that time.

It is important to acknowledge that during this period, hockey was not the primary source of income for the players involved. Their participation in these teams was often driven by a genuine love for the sport rather than financial gain. The reward of receiving a buffet ticket and a beer highlights the amateur nature of these teams and the limited resources available to support them.

Nonetheless, the existence of these early organized teams and their dedication to the game provided a foundation for the growth of hockey in Las Vegas. They played a crucial role in laying the groundwork for the sport's development and building a community of hockey enthusiasts in the city.

These early teams, despite the challenges they faced, contributed to the overall progression of hockey in Las Vegas and set the stage for future endeavors.

Their passion and dedication to the game helped pave the way for the emergence of more structured and professional hockey organizations in the city in subsequent years.

Las Vegas Gamblers
(California-Nevada Hockey League, 1968-71)

It didn't come with the fanfare that accompanied this city's entry into the NHL, but hockey in this city dates all the way back to 1968. Call it semi-pro, if you will, but the rag-tag group of hockey buffs formed their own team and joined a league of other like teams to play a sport they grew up with elsewhere starting in 1968.

That year, the Las Vegas Gamblers, aka Nevada Gamblers, began as a senior amateur team but grew into a semi-pro squad that played in the California-Nevada Hockey League (although rumors persist that many of these players were unpaid, which would negate its semi-pro transition).

That same league later morphed into the Pacific Southwest Hockey League and then into the West Coast Hockey League. An unaffiliated version of the team played on before disbanding in the mid-1990s.

Before it ceased to exist, this league, throughout all its modifications, housed two separate Las Vegas franchises, as well as three in Reno (the Gamblers, Renegades, and an early version of the Aces).

Enter: The Ice Palace

The story of hockey in Las Vegas starts with an ice rink.

The rink was called the International Ice Palace, and it was built in the late 1960s in the Commercial Center strip mall about eight blocks east of the Sahara Hotel and Casino.

"And the rink, as I was told, was built by the Teamsters union — or with Teamsters union money," Brian Bulmer told Martin Kessler during a podcast back in 2018.

For Vegas historians, this comes as no surprise.

"Jimmy Hoffa, the head of the Teamsters union in the late '50s, was tied to organized crime — there's really no dispute about that," said Geoff Schumacher, senior director of content for the Mob Museum in Las Vegas. "They sorta came up with this scheme for the Teamsters Union pension fund to be used to hand out loans for construction of casinos and other things in Las Vegas."

No one alive can say for sure whether the mob or Jimmy Hoffa had anything to do with the Teamsters loaning money to build an ice rink in the middle of the desert, but Bulmer offered this:

"All I can say about that is we were told that the rink was built with money enough to have individual seating. But when it was built, it was just bare, aluminum benches," Bulmer said. "So, that money went somewhere, and I don't know where. But that's just part of

Don Woodbury

the history of this town."The Ice Palace did not have individual seats, but it did have a bar overlooking the ice and a regulation-size rink.

The team formed in 1968 and started playing teams from Los Angeles, Salt Lake City, and other nearby cities. The Gamblers had an eclectic roster. They had schoolteachers and bartenders, blackjack and craps dealers. There was a guy who sold booze to the 600-plus bars in town — and eventually, an FBI agent who had come to multiple practices when he wasn't catching bank robbers.

Kessler reported in his podcast that preceded an on-line print article: "But there were a couple of challenges for a hockey team trying to attract a crowd in Las Vegas in the late '60s. First off, there was lots of competition

for people's attention. I asked Don Woodbury, another former Gambler, if the average people in town knew much about the sport when he arrived in Las Vegas.

"Oh, no. They had no idea," he replied.

In 1968, Woodbury was transferred to Las Vegas for his job with Firestone tires. He'd grown up playing junior hockey in the Ottawa Auditorium, which held 7,000 fans and was built for the sport. As for the Las Vegas Ice Palace?

"This wasn't," he said. "I mean, I think hockey was an afterthought."

And when the Gamblers played at home, there was a tradition for the players and fans after every game.

"We'd go upstairs and party with them," Woodbury said.

'Teams Wanted To Come Here'

The International Ice Palace only had room for about a couple thousand fans. That first season, only a few hundred would show up for games.

In the Gamblers' game program, there was a section called "Know Your Hockey," which explained the rules.

But the Gamblers did have some things going for them from the start. With so many young transplants from Canada and the Midwest living in town, the team drew guys who had grown up playing high-level youth hockey.

And then there was this from Kessler's podcast:

"Was it hard for you guys to ever get teams to come visit and play you guys?"

"No. Not at all," Bulmer said.

"They loved to play us," Woodbury said.

"Teams wanted to come here all the time," Bulmer continued. "As soon as they found out it was available, we could pick and choose."

Teams from the Midwest and beyond started coming to Vegas to play on Friday and Saturday nights. But usually, opponents would get to town on Thursday.

"We'd have a party when they arrived at the hotel. I was gonna say no drinking, but you'd know I was lying," Woodbury said.

"Oh, yeah. Get 'em drunk," said Bill Briski, the booze salesman/defenseman on the Gamblers roster. "Get 'em drunk and tell 'em, 'Hey, take it easy on us. We don't have a whole lot here.' And by the time they woke up, they were behind, 5-1."

"We usually won that first game. We usually did," Bulmer said. "So, I have to say that Briski's a pretty smart fellow."

"They thought they were coming out; they were going to do some gambling and drinking, a regular junket. It was a holiday for them, right?" Woodbury said. "But they would get beat, and they would say, 'Oh, God, you guys are really good.'"

'Any Place We Went, We'd Bring The Fans'

The Gamblers won a lot. And they started drawing bigger crowds.

"It just kind of snowballed," Bulmer said.

Sometimes, fans would watch practices. A busload would follow the team to games in Fresno or Reno.

Briski said the bar above the rink would be so packed after games you could barely move. Fans would buy the players drinks — and they'd talk about the game. And it wasn't just limited to the bar at the

Ice Palace.

"Any place we went, we'd bring fans with us," Briski said. "Oh, we had a good time. Yeah. Everybody had a good time."

But while the fans were having a good time, something else was going on.

"Did you notice that over time, the crowds became more knowledgeable about the sport?" Kessler asked Brian Bulmer.

"Oh, absolutely," Bulmer said. "Absolutely, that happened. They knew what was going on. They knew what should be going on — Icing, offside, the penalties. When they thought there was a penalty that should be called, they let the refs know."

Woodbury still remembers one fan — a local chef — who'd catch his eye every game and give a thumbs up or a thumbs down, depending on how he felt.

On at least one occasion, a Gamblers fan tried to fight an opposing player. So, a hockey culture was developing in Las Vegas. But drawing fans wasn't the only way the Gamblers brought the sport to the city.

"We taught so many kids how to skate," Bill Briski said.

"We'd get a folding chair out there and let them push it around the ice," Brian Bulmer said.

Kessler said, "I love the image of you guys as these high-level hockey players — in most other towns, if

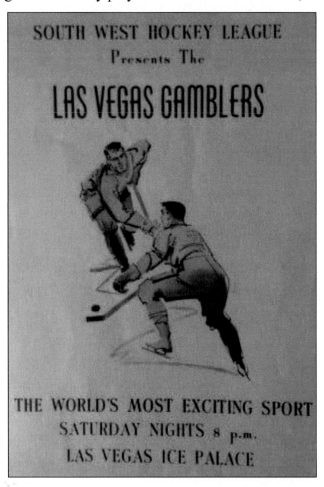

SOUTH WEST HOCKEY LEAGUE
Presents The

LAS VEGAS GAMBLERS

THE WORLD'S MOST EXCITING SPORT
SATURDAY NIGHTS 8 p.m.
LAS VEGAS ICE PALACE

you guys were coaching youth players, it would probably be the cream of the crop. But here you guys are in Las Vegas, literally teaching little kids how to skate,"

"That's exactly it," Bulmer said. "And it was a lot of fun."

"It was more like a community-type thing," Briski said. "And the parents would be in there, and that would help our thing, too. Get the parents and the kids interested in our game."

The podcast aired on June 2, 2018.

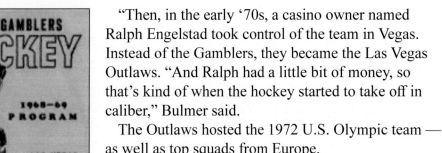

Las Vegas Outlaws
(Independent, 1971-73)

Like the Gamblers before them, the Las Vegas Outlaws' stay on the hockey scene was a short one.

The Outlaws were semi-pro (If they were paid at all), playing independently from a single league against a variety of opponents for two seasons from 1971 to 1973. With this unconventional setup, the Outlaws - who kind of were Outlaws - put together one of the best single-season records of any hockey team in Las Vegas history — the inaugural 1971-72 team went 29-8-4-0.

Their star was a little forward from Lucky Lake, Saskatchewan, named Bryant Bogren, who racked up 30 goals and 67 assists during the team's banner 1971- '72 season.

Brian Bulmer estimates that over the years, he and his teammates taught a few hundred kids in Las Vegas how to skate. He went on to tell Kessler:

"Then, in the early '70s, a casino owner named Ralph Engelstad took control of the team in Vegas. Instead of the Gamblers, they became the Las Vegas Outlaws. "And Ralph had a little bit of money, so that's kind of when the hockey started to take off in caliber," Bulmer said.

The Outlaws hosted the 1972 U.S. Olympic team — as well as top squads from Europe.

"We were really starting to build something," Bulmer said.

"But like lots of attractions in Las Vegas, the hockey team was hot for a couple years — and then it was on the outs."

There are a couple of possible explanations. Briski said the team got into trouble on an overseas trip. (There may have been too much trash talk against the Russians and too many fights in Germany).

Bulmer said the owner of the rink and the owner of the team could not come to an agreement.

"The rink wasn't available to us anymore," he said. "And Ralph Engelstad actually started to build his own rink. But it never turned out. And hockey just died right there."

Engelstad was later given the largest fine to date from the Nevada Gaming Commission for hosting Nazi parties regaled in Nazi garb with an ample collection of Nazi memorabilia in his hotel.

The Outlaws folded after the '74-'75 season.

But even though the team stopped playing, there were still all those adults in town who had come to love the sport and all those kids who had learned to skate.

"I would love to think that some of those people are part of what's out there watching the Golden Knights now," Bulmer told Kessler. "And I hope we left a little bit of enjoyment that helped to build with this."

Chapter 2

Rich Rose and His Impossible Dream

In 1991, Las Vegas would never have been included in the conversation for getting a pro sports team from any of the Big Four leagues of NHL Hockey, NBA Basketball, NFL Football, or Major League Baseball. Vegas had three strikes against it: weather, gambling, and a population base too small to ever support a franchise. Amateur sports teams struggled to survive for decades.

The only professional league foray from the Big Four in Las Vegas was the 11 games the Utah Jazz played in the newly constructed Thomas & Mack Center. On April 5, 1984, Los Angeles Lakers star Kareem Abdul-Jabbar became the NBA's all-time scoring leader against the Jazz in Las Vegas, with Utah losing 129-115. The Utah Jazz stay lasted until their new arena was built. Vegas was booked out of desperation, and only exhibition basketball games were played thereafter.

The population base in the late 1980s was roughly 350,000 people. Then came a population explosion, with Vegas becoming the most desired objective for relocation of families and businesses in the United States.

As the landscape of the Las Vegas Strip began to expand, casinos for "Locals" in neighborhoods sprung up like blooming flowers after a desert rain. With the population boom came pioneers of small professional sports teams that failed miserably. They were fun to watch, but only AAA baseball made an impact.

Rich Rose

Why Not Vegas?

Las Vegas was the Boxing Capital of the World, but the shadiness that surrounded the sport was evident. Betting on boxing was big business but wagering on Big 4 sports other than football was in its infantile stage. Sports gambling cast a pall on the city, and any affiliation outside Nevada was met with solid resistance.

Pro sports leagues loathed the thought of any affiliation with wagering. The 1919 Black Sox scandal slapped a huge blemish on the game of baseball.

College basketball betting scandals cast ugly aspersions on the amateur game. Sports games needed to be viewed as clean, and Vegas was viewed as a dirty business despite the fact every good bar in any big city had its own bookie. Change was slow to come back in 1991.

Enter Caesars Palace

Caesars Palace was the numero uno destination for small and large fights. Small fights were held in the Pavilion in the rear of the property, which seated 2,600 fans when filled.

For the mega fights, stands were brought in the back of the property to construct a boxing arena that could host 18,000 fans, most of them casino customers, for the biggest bouts, most heavyweight encounters. The back of Caesars also hosted the Formula I Gran Prix and professional tennis with the likes of Jimmy Connors, Bjorn Borg and Andre Agassi. Other amateur and pro events included weightlifting, billiards, gymnastics and Olympic skating exhibitions. Those events were not posted on casino sports betting boards, making boxing the only sport in Vegas that had odds posted for wagering on events in Nevada.

La, La, La, La Lola

When Rich Rose took the job in the entertainment Division at Caesars World International in Los Angeles, he had his sights set on an outdoor hockey game to go with the array of sports already in existence. An avid New York Rangers fan, Rose envisioned an NHL game on the Caesars Palace property with his favorite team. He didn't advertise or boast of his intentions; he would have been locked up.

"No question about when I got the job with Henry Gluck and Terri Lanni, that was one of three things I wanted to do," Rose recalls. "I had the pleasure to be part of the birth of professional hockey in Las Vegas, and it took almost three years to get the game. The NHL didn't want anything to do with Vegas, and I had nowhere to begin."

Leave it to Rose to take on the monumental task of luring a reckless, speculative venture to the classiest hotel/casino in the land.

John Ziegler was president of the NHL at the time, and he despised Vegas because of the stigma of gambling, and he didn't want aspersions cast upon any NHL contest. Undeterred, Rose took his shot by calling the league office to make his first inquiry. He didn't specifically call for Ziegler and didn't know where to begin.

Rose's first call to the league office was taken by the receptionist, who is only remembered as Lola, who transferred the call to the sponsorships department, headed up by Larry Flatow.

"Rich called the League Office one day," Flatow recalled. "I forgot exactly when it was. We had a receptionist named Lola, who was used to screening all sorts of calls and figuring out, you know, who should get this one and who should get that one. And I was the vice president for sponsorships of the league. And so, she thought immediately that the call was a sponsor-related kind of a thing."

Getting through to the president was impossible and, as it turns out, would have been fatal.

"I didn't even know who Rich was," Flatow said. "I answered the phone, and he introduced himself and told me what his plan was. So that's how I got involved. I was the random recipient of Lola's to receive that call instead of someone else. Of all the other people that call could have gone to, frankly, I don't know who would have taken it seriously or who would have been interested in helping Rich and encouraging him. I think many of the other people probably would have just said, 'no thanks.'"

Flatow told Rose that each NHL team had the autonomy to create its own exhibition schedule. The NHL wanted nothing to do with the exhibition season. Rose thought the Los Angeles Kings would be the biggest draw because of their proximity to Vegas and the fact they had the biggest draw the sport had ever seen – Wayne Gretzky.

"So, I'm glad the call went to me 'cause I think that helped facilitate it happening," Flatow said.

Flatow's first thoughts when Rose pitched it were the technical challenges.

"It's not the cost of freezing a rink on a parking lot in Vegas, but when it's 90 degrees out, that would make it a challenge.

"He was certain he could do it," Flatow said of Rose. "He was very self-assured. He obviously knew everything behind the scenes that was involved in arranging the rink setup. He probably had more understanding of the technical side of it, but I had no idea. I mean, it just seemed improbable. Big challenges and big costs."

Rose asked Flatow if he should talk to Ziegler before talking to the Kings.

"Flatow took my call," Rose said. "He said, 'Here's my suggestion if you wanna get it done. If you want to do this, I would get ahold of Bruce McNall.'"

"I told him that that was exactly the wrong thing to do," Flatow said of calling Ziegler. "And I steered him into doing the right thing, which ultimately made this happen. I told him the way to get this done (go directly to the Kings). If he had reached Ziegler, this would have died right there. Back then, if you talked professional sports and casinos in the same sentence, you'd have no shot."

Flatow worked for the NHL for eight years, and yet he had no hockey background, only a pro sports marketing background.

"I had a professional sports background. Business-wise, I never played hockey. But I'd been doing this a long time," Flatow said. "I worked for the NBA, I worked for the Major Indoor Soccer League. I've done a number of different marketing ventures and similar events."

Flatow saw the promise of an outdoor event.

"This came together almost by itself," Flatow said. "The other thing I said to Rich was make this a preseason game. I think his idea was to try to play a regular season game there, and I said, 'You know, that'll never happen.' But teams have complete preseason control. Teams can control where they play their preseason games and how many of them to do. Many, many teams play preseason games other than in their NHL arena because they wanna expose the game to people in other parts of their territory. Rich picked up the puck from there and did everything. I can't take any credit for having done this once he took the ideas that I gave him. Rich did everything else."

Rose knew he needed the Kings for proximity and their drawing power, thanks to the game's best player.

"The league struggled to create a fan base and a major sport in the United States, especially the West, despite how popular it was in Canada," Flatow recalled. "And you remember that in the summer of 1988, some guy named Wayne Gretzky got traded to the Los Angeles Kings, and suddenly everything is different, right? You knew in the United States, Wayne was gonna be the leader of the band. Bruce McNall was celebrated as the man who made that happen. I don't know if genius is the right word, but he's the guy who pulled it off. He was the guy who got Wayne Gretzky away from the team that had won four Stanley Cups. Bruce was not angelic, you know, but Bruce was the shining new thinker in the league."

McNall Gets The Call

"Bruce was always in a sort of an exalted position where John Ziegler was concerned," Flatow recalled. "John was always deferential to the team owners anyway. Had Rich gone straight to John, he would have said no, that's not our business. We can't do that. We can't do any visual things with individual teams. You know, sorry. And that would have been the end of the conversation. So, I just told him, I said, 'Rich, this is the way to get this done. Call Bruce.'"

Rose's next call was to the Kings brass and Mc-Nall. Rose was able to convince the Kings' executive vice-president, Roy Mlakar, and then McNall.

Bruce Patrick McNall, born April 17, 1950, was a thoroughbred racehorse owner and sports executive. He claimed to have made his initial fortune as a coin collector. However, Metropolitan Museum of Art director Thomas Hoving claimed he made a ton of money as he smuggled art antiquities as the partner of Robert E. Hecht. In the 1980s, McNall produced several Hollywood movies, including The Manhattan Project and Weekend at Bernie's. He was charismatic and just what the NHL needed on the West Coast.

McNall bought a 25 percent stake in the Kings from Jerry Buss in 1986 and bought an additional 24 percent in 1987 to become the team's largest shareholder. He was named the team president that September and purchased Buss' remaining shares in March 1988. He stunned the sports world on Aug. 9, 1988, when he acquired the NHL's biggest star along with Marty McSorley and Mike Krushelnyski from the Edmonton Oilers for Jimmy Carson, Martin Gelinas, three first-round draft choices and $15 million. McNall raised Gretzky's annual salary from less than $1 million to $3 million, which, in turn, triggered a dramatic rise in NHL salaries throughout the 1990s.

In 1992, McNall was elected chairman of the NHL Board of Governors, the league's second-highest post.

"McNall was a Golden Boy who was gonna get almost whatever he wanted," Flatow said. "Vegas is obviously very close to L.A. and arguably, in those days, was their best marketplace. The pieces were all there. We have Wayne Gretzky in L.A. and the league started to have a national impact. We had a Golden Boy owner who basically could get anything he wanted. So, we had justification in that sense because of what he had done three years earlier. An active leader of the new wing of the NHL, John was gonna say yes to him, and again, the rest is history."

"At first, McNall looked at me like I was crazy," Rose said. "I said, 'Look, we will pay you.' By the time we consulted an hour and 40 minutes later, he was on board and got excited about it," Rose said. "I said, 'We will make this a national thing of national interest.'

"He said you can bring your own opponent, although selfishly, I would love it to be the New York Rangers. He said it would be great if we got the Rangers."

After securing the Kings with a $200,000 enticement, Flatow helped Rose contact the Rangers, who agreed to play, and the event was scheduled for September 27, 1991.

"You know, New York versus L.A. always stirs national interest," Flatow said. "They are obviously, you know, one of the Original Six. Get the Rangers. And so, I knew I had to have them."

Rose grew up in New York playing pond hockey, and the Original Six team was his first choice.

"Neil Smith is one of my best friends," Rose said. "Neill was president of the Rangers at that time, and he said yes."

Neil Smith originally was a Canadian ice hockey broadcaster born in 1954 and was the general manager of both the New York Rangers from 1989 to 2000 and (briefly) the New York Islanders in 2006. He was also

the owner and head coach of the Johnstown Chiefs of the ECHL.

Becoming the first venue to host an outdoor hockey game was a goal come true for Rose. He got it sanctioned by the national league without having to go through Ziegler. Never mind that it was a scorching 90 degrees or more in September. Forget about it being in Sin City.

"Because the teams had the ability to essentially dictate where they played preseason games and on what financial circumstances and so on, basically he did the rest," Flatow said. "But no one in the league office really believed the game was gonna go off from so many directions, including even internally at Caesars. But the Kings brought some kid named Gretzky to L.A., and McNall's had the power and influence to do it."

Game on? Not yet. Rose had to sell it to Caesars management. He had to convince the Caesars hierarchy, starting with Caesars Entertainment kingpin Terry Lanni.

Lanni joined Caesars World in January 1977 as Chief Financial Officer, was named Senior Vice President in April 1978, and was elected Executive Vice President in December 1979. He was a senior executive of Caesars World, Inc. for 18 years, serving as president and Chief Operating Officer and a member

of the Board of Directors from April 1981 to February 1995. He died of cancer in 2011.

"I went back to the office, and I told everyone, including Terry," Rose said. "I said these guys are in. They wanna do it. And so, they had to go out and do the numbers."

The numbers meant seeing if the game would draw VIPs and the public after expenses.

Rose says the game was the biggest feather in his event production hat.

"For me, of the 10 years that I was at Caesars, I'd take back everything I've ever done just to have that event," Rose said. "I've been fortunate to work with great people and have a lot of opportunities. Of everything I've ever done, this was my most satisfying thing of all."

Vegas and professional ice hockey were now intermingling.

"I'm occasionally in touch with Rich, and I tell him to this day that he has really big balls," Flatow said. "I mean, I don't know if he was putting his job on the line or what his circumstances were, but that was a great thing to try to pull off. I would say yes, it was rather risky."

But would that risk pay off?

ON SEPT. 27, CAESARS PALACE WILL OFFICIALLY ENTER THE ICE AGE.

L.A. KINGS FEATURING WAYNE GRETZKY VS. N.Y. RANGERS, 7:30 PM

Hockey. Outdoors. In the desert. You'll see it for the first time ever in Las Vegas when the Home of Champions presents 'Fire on Ice.' The Los Angeles Kings meet the highflying New York Rangers in an NHL exhibition, Friday Sept. 27th in Caesars' Outdoor Stadium. Tickets start at just $20. Call 731-7865. But do it now. Or else you could be left out in the cold.

CAESARS PALACE
FIRE ON ICE

Chapter 3
We Three Kings

L.A. Kings Owner Bruce McNall knew that in order to put hockey on the map in California, he needed to acquire the best player to ever put on skates. The Edmonton Oilers could no longer afford to pay The Great One, and McNall paid a King's ransom for him.

When Kings management broke it to The Great One that he was going to play outdoors in Vegas in the heat of September, the news was met with a healthy dose of skepticism. The National Hockey League had never had an outdoor hockey game, and a game in the desert was unfathomable.

Having Wayne Gretzky and his four Stanley Cups in five years was a dream come true for Rich Rose. For Gretzky, it was a shock when informed that he was playing a game in Vegas outside.

"I can remember when they told me we were going to play there," Gretzky said on a TNT broadcast during the 2023 Stanley Cup. "And I said, 'Are you guys crazy? This is never going to work.'"

The game was not without its problems and surprises.

Here Come the Kings

Caesars Palace was led at the time by President Dan Reichartz, a hard-nosed, no-nonsense and highly respected leader known for a stern look. Reichartz had hired Phil Cooper months earlier to replace long-running Don Gulielmino as Vice President of Public Relations, one of the most coveted jobs in the city. No one had more juice in town than the head of PR at Caesars.

Cooper was a surprise hire for the position, having come from the restaurant business in Chicago with no casino experience. He did, however, have a flair for marketing and a staff to pull off such a challenging task. Normally, his Director of Public Relations, Debbie Munch, would have been tasked as the lead for the event. Munch was the Queen of Boxing, and no one promoted a fight, or any other event, better than she did. Any opening, any movie shoot, and anything involving the media was led by Munch. She was the

best in the city and knew every media member.

The oddity about Munch was that she was a classically trained musician. She was surely no jock-type and didn't know beans about hockey. Then came the chance of a lifetime for Richard Gubbe.

Gubbe got his first break when Robbie Knievel wanted to pay homage to his father Evel and jumped the Caesars Palace fountains in 1989. The jump took place 22 years after Evel Knievel failed to land safely in 1967 and crashed in a memorable and painful fashion.

"The top brass at Caesars decided to give me the event because it was so risky," Gubbe says. "I honestly believe that they thought the event would fail, and no one wanted to go in front of the international media on TV if Robbie crashed and died. I got the event by default."

Robbie Knievel landed safely and became the first to successfully jump the fountains. Following the jump, Knievel stated, "That was for you, Dad."

"Every day Robbie would go out and move the ramps one way and the next day move them back," Gubbe recalled. "He was heckled by local motorcycle daredevils, and we even had to get a restraining order against Johnnie Airtime. The event became so large we had to get extra fencing the day before in anticipation of a larger-than-expected crowd. More than 50,000 people jammed the front of Caesars. Robbie said that if he made the jump and walked away with his $1 million prize, he would never jump again. A few weeks later, he jumped a row of busses in Hawaii."

Having a large worldwide event under his belt helped him land the Kings-Rangers game, and the brass knew Gubbe was formerly a hockey goalie at the amateur level.

"My knowledge of the game certainly helped land me the Event Coordinator's position," Gubbe said. "After all, Phil Cooper and I were both from Chicago and avid hockey fans. But I think the scenario that the event could fail, and Debbie Munch wanted nothing to do with that, certainly helped. Only a few knew how

The rink behind Caesars is tested two days before the game.
Dave Taylor, below left, and Larry Robinson in promo cards.

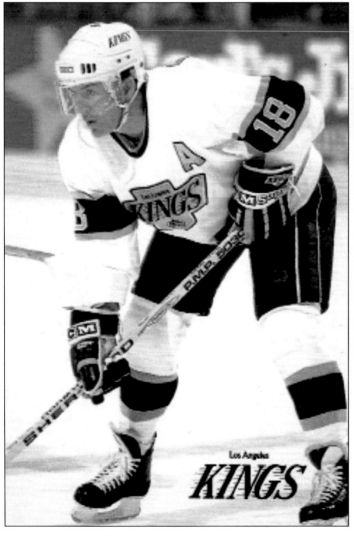 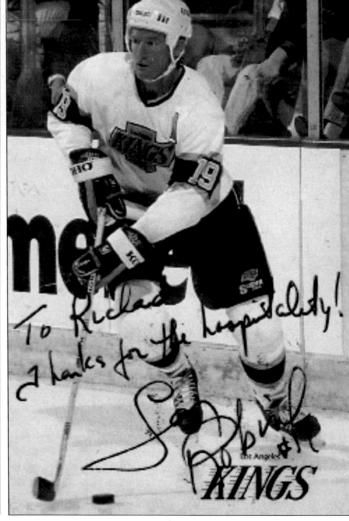

close the event actually came from getting axed."

Part of the agreement to host the game involved three Kings to help promote the game the week of the event, and one of them had to be Gretzky.

Five times between 1981-82 and 1986–87, Gretzky led the NHL in goals scored and he won a total of 9 MVP awards in his career. The Oilers also won the Stanley Cup with Gretzky three additional times – in 1985, 1987 and 1988. Between 1982 and 1985, the Oilers averaged 423 goals a season when no previous team had scored 400, and Gretzky, on his own, had averaged 207 points when no player before had scored more than 152 in one year.

On Aug. 9, 1988, in a move that put West Coast hockey on the map, the Oilers traded Gretzky along with Marty McSorley and Mike Krushelnyski to the Kings for Jimmy Carson, Martin Gélinas, $15 million in cash and the Kings' first-round draft picks in 1989, 1991 and 1993.

In 1990, the Associated Press named Gretzky Male Athlete of the Decade. Gretzky's first season in Los Angeles saw a marked increase in attendance and fan interest in a state not previously known for following hockey. The Kings now boasted of numerous sellouts and many credit Gretzky's arrival with putting non-traditional American hockey markets on the NHL map.

The other two selected for the outdoor game were superstars in their own right – fan favorite Dave Taylor, who endured many fruitless seasons with the Kings, and Larry Robinson, a former Stanley Cup Winner.

Before coming to the Kings, Robinson's peak years were 1976-1977 to 1980-1981, although he had a strong comeback season at age 34 in 1985-1986 when he was again named to the second all-star team and scored 82 points, just three shy of his career high of 85 (1976–1977). Robinson won the James Norris Memorial Trophy twice (1976-1977 and 1979-1980) as the league's most outstanding defenseman and won the Conn Smythe Trophy as the most valuable player of the 1978 playoffs. He was named to the league's first and second all-star teams three times each. Robinson was a dominant player whose talent and leadership helped lead the Canadiens to six Stanley Cups.

During his career, Robinson played in 10 of the league's All-Star games and ended his 20-year career having scored 208 goals, 750 assists, and 958 regular-season points, as well as 144 points in 227 playoff games, a distinctive achievement for a defenseman. He holds an astounding career plus-minus rating of +730, the NHL career record, including an overwhelming +120 in 1976-1977 (second only to Bobby Orr's

record of +124 in 1970-1971. Together with Nicklas Lidstrom, Robinson holds the NHL record for most consecutive playoff seasons with 20, 17 of them with the Canadiens. He then went on to coach the New Jersey Devils to two Stanley Cups and coached the Kings in between. In 1995, he was inducted into the Hockey Hall of Fame.

Taylor played in the NHL with the Kings from 1977 to 1994. He played in the 1993 Stanley Cup Finals with the Kings. Following his playing career, he served as the Kings' general manager from 1997 to 2006. A nicer guy in hockey never existed, except for Gretzky.

Taylor was a member of the famous Triple Crown Line along with Hall of Fame center Marcel Dionne and left winger Charlie Simmer. In the 1980-1981 season, all three scored more than 100 points with the Kings with Dionne and Simmer scoring 135 and 105 points, respectively, and Taylor scoring 112 points to record the best season of his career. The Kings have retired #18 in his honor.

Caesars Palace now had the best hockey trio to make a splash before the game.

Cooper and Caesars then went to work on marketing.

"Everything from putting out the VIP invitation with a puck that we sent out that was very exclusive to the Caesars Palace customer," Cooper said. "I think I've still got about 40 of them somewhere. If I didn't come out of there with 20 of everything from every event, you know, I wasn't doing my job to preserve the event in the archives of Caesars."

'I Want to Play with the People'

After the ink had dried on the contracts in June, prior to the event with the Kings and Rangers, the game was turned over to the staff at Caesars Palace on Las Vegas Boulevard. Caesars didn't have a ton of access to the threesome, but just having Gretzky on property created a buzz for the upcoming game.

When the three Kings arrived earlier in the week, there was a meeting in Reichartz's office with Cooper, Gubbe, Rose and Gretzky.

"I remember when Dan offered Wayne the private casino reserved only for the highest of high rollers," Cooper recalled. Adorned with Roman statuary and expensive artwork in the classic Caesars setting of the Palace Court Casino, the private venue was home to a few blackjack and craps tables along with a roulette table amidst the lavish surroundings. Only gaming whales and celebrity VIPs were allowed access to the Palace Court, and Caesars had to make special arrangements just to open the venue.

Gretzky declined the invitation.

Caesars Event Coordinator Richard Gubbe poses with The Great One a few days before the game.

"I want to play with the people," Gretzky said. "I want to be in the real action with everyone else."

"It was actually right at the end of the meeting as everybody was leaving. So yeah, Gretzky said no," Rose recalled. "I remember walking through the Forum Casino afterward. And he was sitting at a blackjack table. I've dealt with athletes in virtually every sport. And they were excited to be there 'cause they were a part of the energy the Forum offered."

Cooper remembers the meeting well.

"I remember the meeting that we had in Dan's (Reichartz) office. It was just me, you. Bruce and Wayne in the office," Cooper said. "It was actually me asking Dan if Wayne could have a private casino. Gretzky wanted to gamble but not by himself in the Palace Court. Yeah, he wouldn't do it. You know, he was not a showman, but he said he wanted to play with the people. And that's what he did, play blackjack with the people."

Cooper dealt with McNall and Gretzky often while they were on the property.

"I really did deal with Bruce a lot," Cooper said. "That wasn't the fun part. But, I mean, the fun part was Gretzky being in the Palace all week. So that was great. I remember having breakfast with Gretzky and (wife) Janet in Cafe Roma, and Gretzky was telling me how full of shit the guy was. But here he was, the owner with a crapload of money that he gave Gretzky."

Fun and Gaming

Although many of the Kings gambled that week, when Kelley Hrudey came in, he did not.

"When I first heard of the game, I was certainly in favor of it," Hrudey said in 2023. "But I'm not a gambler; I don't gamble at all. But when I was with

my teammates and some of the Rangers, we strolled through the casino. It was just jammed. We hit the town and were fascinated by the Strip at night."

While many of the players hit the tables, the NHL detested gambling, which was why Vegas had never come close to hosting an event of any kind. The odds were prohibitive. Caesars honored that and kept the game off the board.

"We didn't put the game up in the Caesars Sports Book," Rose said. "They wouldn't let us put the game on the board. There was no line on the game, but who cared? I mean, it made such a statement."

For Rose, having the game in town was satisfying enough.

"The game was one more thing to add to a long list of my signings that included Circus of the Stars, all the movies, all the gigs with entertainers that Caesars Palace had done and the great fights over the years. This was one more blue ribbon."

Cooper said Caesars wanted to show the world that the Palace could put on a legitimate event in a Big $ Sport.

"Back then, it was staking your reputation on every event we produced. We were trying to change the dynamic when pro sports were above it all and so squeaky clean," Cooper said. "Whether it was NHL Hockey or Davis Cup, or tennis matches with Bjorn Borg and Jimmy Connors, it was all legit."

The Rink

The Boxing Capitol of the World outdoor venue was about to employ the first outdoor hockey rink.

Caesars had hosted The War and Sugar Ray Leonard in a classic fight in 1989, and Thomas Hearns faced Virgil Hill in June of 1991, just three months prior to

Larry Robinson picks up a future star during the Amateur Skate the night before the big game.

Phil Cooper of Caesars Palace and radio personality Mike O'Brian in the old days.

the scheduled game with the Kings and Rangers in the outdoor venue. That venue had to be totally transformed into a passable ice rink with boards that met the standards of the NHL and the players themselves.

The company called upon to pull off the miracle was Ice Systems of America owned and operated by brothers Bob and Don May, who were recommended by the NHL.

The ice-making technology then wasn't near what it is today, but the May Brothers guaranteed Rose it could be done in the desert in September when temperatures easily reached 90 degrees or higher.

There was barely room in the back parking lot to have enough space for a regulation rink. There was also barely room to fit in stands to house nearly 14,000 fans.

"We had to reconfigure the outdoor venue, the outdoor arena," Rose said. "We had to move the north and south grandstands back, and we only had 192 feet, which was OK despite being short of 200 feet. Remember, the old Chicago Stadium was 180 feet long. Boston Garden was 186, so at 192, we were fine. It was a preseason game. Nobody cared anyway about a few extra feet, but that's as far as we could get and still have the stands."

The temporary rink cost $135,000 to erect, and the ice was ready two days prior to the event. The ice was laid down under the direction of Michael Rzechula and Robert Krolak from ITI (aka Ice Rink Supply). According to May, the outside ice rink in Las Vegas was "a big challenge," using three times the refrigeration equipment as one would for a regular rink. Fabric strips were laid into the ice as opposed to the usual painted stripes.

"This was Tuesday night when we first made the ice," Rose said. "There was a new technology for what I remember about the freon that had never been done before. They laid the pipes the way they were in a normal arena. May said the only problem we could have would be the wind. If we don't get any wind, we're going to have a perfect sheet of ice. There was no wind to speak of that week."

The temperatures cooled down at night during the week, and there was a blanket over the ice for the daylight sun.

"We had the green light from the NHL," Rose said. "So many people said that I couldn't do it. Not gonna happen. The crew members were all part of hockey history.

"It was something no one had done," Rose said of Ice Systems. "I mean, I'm sure virtually everybody who was going to play that night had skated outdoors sometime growing up, just not in temperatures that hot."

The Amateur Skate

The first time NHL players stepped onto an ice surface in Las Vegas was the night before the game came during an amateur skate with local sports celebrities and local youth players. The first two players who were paid to play in Vegas were Larry Robinson and Dave Taylor from the Los Angeles Kings.

The event was held to help promote amateur hockey in Las Vegas, especially at the level of youth hockey. The week was part of the agreement the Kings made with Caesars to help promote the event.

The event wasn't publicized on radio or TV. A select crew of media members were chosen who Caesars execs knew they could skate. The ice was full of small children, ages 5 to 10. The nighttime setting had perfect weather. The outer rim around the boards of the arena were lined with executives from Caesars, and family and staff of the Kings, and a few employees from Caesars and the ice makers. Randy Huartson, who owned the only hockey store in town, provided the youngest kids and fitted them with some equipment. He was instrumental in building adult and youth amateur hockey at the Santa Fe Hotel/Casino. He helped supply kids and the adults with equipment to play in the first organized Santa Fe leagues. He died prematurely of cancer in 2013.

"We were just talking, and I had an idea that we wanted to get the community involved and get as much free press as we could," Cooper said. "So, we got DJs, press people, and we got young amateur players in hockey gear thanks to Randy. So, was it a little of everything. We had Gubbe go live dressed in his goalie equipment," Cooper said. "We had (radio personality) Mike O'Brian and (Las Vegas Sun sportswriter) Steve Carp skating out with a bunch of young kids in a skate around. It was just an amazing skate around. It also was VIP treatment for a few casino customers who were looking on."

"I can remember passing the puck around with Dave Taylor," Carp said. "No one else in the media knew how to skate, so it was just the three of us."

The whole amateur skate was about the kids, but the adults were just as thrilled.

O'Brian, longtime radio morning show host, showed he had some skills.

"It was a big thrill for me to be out there," O'Brian said. "Only Caesars could have pulled that off. That's what Caesars did back then. 'Let's just build a Grand Prix racetrack around Caesars Palace.' They did it. So, when the idea about hockey came up, I remember some of the people said, 'Are you crazy?' It was awesome as it happened. And the night before the game, we skated and skated. I thought it was awesome because growing up, I played hockey outside. The ice was great and the rink was perfect. And it was so cool to be skating outside. In what people call, of course, the desert with these professional hockey guys, I was in heaven. Dave was one of my guys I got to work with. Randy Huartson, up at the hockey store, outfitted a lot of the kids and me. That was a career highlight for me."

After a fun hour and a half or more, the ice slowly started to clear, leaving two skaters on the ice.

"Larry Robinson and I, we were teasing each other all week because he knew I had played goal," Gubbe recalled. "He said things like, 'Oh, you think you're a goalie? You think you're any good? I'm gonna tear you up when I get you out there.'"

The banter continued.

"I said, you know, come Thursday night, it's gonna be you and me and I'm gonna stone you. And he said, 'Yeah, we'll see.' Well, we didn't think much of it during the event and never saw each other during the event. He was at the other end of the rink working with the kids. We all were, and the skate went on. At the end of the night, the last two people on the ice were me and Larry Robinson.

"We had forgotten about all the banter, but as fate would have it, we were the last two people on the ice," Gubbe recalled. "I called out to him and there was a puck sitting at center ice. He took a puck at center ice and came down like a penalty shot."

"We were all standing and watching," Cooper said.

"Larry came flying down and shoots shot a wrist shot, trying to go over my glove hand to embarrass me on my glove side," Gubbe said. "And I snatched it out of the air and showed it to him. I just happened to guess right."

"I remember I could see you turning right around and showing it to him," Cooper said. "Then he skated off after one shot."

"Well, he got so pissed off, they locked me out of the locker room," Gubbe said. "One of the Kings answered when I pounded on the door. He said, 'Yeah, you're not gonna be able to change in here. Larry is mad. Go somewhere else.' And they were, of course, just teasing. I had to wait until they were all dressed. But it was all just fun. He wasn't mad at me; he was just playing with me. But those guys, the reason I say this is that they were so cooperative. You know, they cared about the amateur skate almost as much as they did about the game."

The entire week went smoothly.

"You don't always see that out of pro athletes," Gubbe said. "I have interviewed many pro greats as a sportswriter and PR specialist, and the Three Kings were fun-loving and cooperative. But I have that puck right next to the Caesars VIP puck. I've carried that puck with me my whole life."

Richard Gubbe in goal during the amateur skate.

"Did he sign it?" Cooper asked.

"I didn't have the nerve to ask," Gubbe said. "I wish to God I could have gotten him to sign it."

The Amateur Skate was more than just a couple of hours of fun. The event had lasting memories around Caesars Palace, where event memories in the form of posters and pictures hung on every wall.

"I had that famous picture of Larry Robinson picking up that junior mini hockey player hanging in my office after that," Cooper said. "That was such a great shot. I had it on my wall in my office until I left."

Although not in the annals of greatest events ever at Caesars, it was the start of pro players hitting the ice in the desert.

"We orchestrated the Amateur Skate to get a lot of press and we had live news cameras there for the night just to promote the hockey game," Cooper said. "But the goal that night was for the kids to have fun. It was just an amazing time."

"But the fact that you were skating in Vegas outside with temperatures in the mid-80s. That was pretty amazing," O'Brian said.

The game and the Skate the night before left a big impression on Taylor. "Years later, I went out to a hockey game in Phoenix with my family," O'Brian recalled in 2023. "And it just so happened Dave Taylor was part of the broadcast. And as I walked by him. I said, 'Mr. Taylor, I just want to introduce myself. You don't know me. I'm Michael O'Brian, and I do radio in Vegas. I skated with you on the ice in the back of Caesars Palace back in the early '90s.' And he looked at me and his eyes just lit up.

"He turned to his broadcast partner, and he started telling the story behind the game in great detail. He said, 'Caesars Palace put up this unbelievable ice rink. We're playing hockey against New York and there's grasshoppers on the rink (see next chapter) and it's hot, but the ice was great.'

"I just stood there. Like, wow, he remembers that! With everything that he did in his career, he remembers that like it was yesterday? It made me feel so good that Vegas had a place in his heart. If you were living or working here at Caesars at that time and got to be a part of that in any way, shape or form or were part of the crowd that watched the game, you were part of an amazing event. You know, and this is so cheesey to say it, but Richard, you'll get this because you've been in Vegas for a long time. It was such a Vegas thing to do. And it was just odd seeing people in shorts and T-shirts watching a hockey game."

Steve Carp, Mike O'Brian and Richard Gubbe became big fans of Dave Taylor.

Chapter 4
Outdoor Madness

After a successful Amateur Skate the night before, the stage was set for a big day.

"My job was to make sure all went smoothly," Caesars Public Relations Coordinator Richard Gubbe recalled. "All was rather quiet. The day brought the usual 'sunny day in paradise' that we were accustomed to. There was nary a cloud in the sky and typical hot September temperatures."

Then all hell rained down.

"I was in my office, and I got a call shortly after noon saying 'you need to go down to the rink. Something happened.'"

To shield the rink from the blistering sun, a sun-filtering tarp that was installed to avoid the direct heat was laying on the ice, or what was the ice and was now a large pool of water. One of the rinkmaster's employees had lowered the tarp for some unknown reason. Word spread quickly, and Bob May and Rich Rose arrived on the scene.

"It was 12:30 when the crew was supposed to come down and only one guy showed up, and he cut all the ropes so that the heat blanket dropped on the ice," Rose said.

Bob May was furious. What was supposed to be his biggest success he had as an ice maker was now a lake. The heat index was about 110 that day, but May was hotter than that.

"I never heard someone swear so much in my life," Gubbe said. "After the yelling died down, I called Bob over for a private conversation."

May then began the biggest and quickest recovery ever. The game was in doubt.

"Because I was the guy who would have to go in front of TV cameras and explain why and how such a debacle had occurred, I asked May if it would be fixed or not," Gubbe said. "He assured me that it would be ice again in a timely manner."

It took 90 minutes just to raise the tarp, raising fears that irreparable damage had been done.

"A normal NHL rink is 18 degrees," Rose said. "We had set ours at 11 degrees."

May and his crew put the ice together in less than three hours. The crew used crepe paper to establish the lines instead of the originally designed paint.

"They dropped the ice temperature to 3 degrees, and we prayed," Rose said. "That was our only hope."

Some furious restoration action by a Zamboni to restore a smooth surface saved the night and made the ice smooth and playable, but the gametime was delayed.

"It probably helped that the ice on the Caesars rink was two inches thick," Rose said. "It was twice the thickness of regular NHL playing surfaces. By five o'clock, we had enough ice to send the Zamboni out. I remember it all too well. They were beside themselves, but to their credit, they worked a miracle."

Pre-Game Jitters

When Caesars has a big event that needs promotion because a lot of seats need to be sold to tourists, the responsibility rests primarily with the event coordinator. Promotion involves press events, the purchasing of tourist magazine covers and press releases to the media. Because the Amateur Skate provided some local exposure, the hockey event relied on magazine covers and articles to reach the tourists who arrived on the day or days prior to the event. Presales for the game were light, and executives were worried about filling the stands for a hockey event that had never happened before this event.

"My job was to put butts in the seats, and the seats weren't going all that quickly," Gubbe recalled. "Then I got word of a near-riot in the Olympic Casino where the box office was for this event. Imagine, I got in trouble because everyone wanted their tickets all at once. VIPs and tourists all came in the two hours before the event. Executives may have been a bit rankled, but I secured a reputation as a solid event promoter with a near-sellout."

Hockey Night In Vegas

Rose recalls that when his staff came over from Los Angeles on the day of the game, the flight was packed with Kings fans.

"The game became a big deal and the response from Southern California was great," Rose said.

The boards featured rotating and lit advertising panels, a concept using technology that was still in its infancy but later implemented in many NHL arenas. In-board advertisers included Toyota, Target, ITT Sheraton, Budweiser, Thrifty Car Rental and Upper Deck trading cards.

The tarp drop caused the delay of the start, and there was no pregame skate other than the obligatory skate-around when the teams came out before the game.

"If you look back, if you see a tape of the game, the lighting was horrible, and we had the three towers," Rose said. "If we were doing it today, we'd have three to four times the light. But it didn't matter. Everybody was so into it."

Kelly Hrudey wore a goalie cam during the outdoor game at Caesars Palace.

Calling the game for Prime Ticket cable sports that night was the longtime Los Angeles Kings' broadcast team of Bob Miller and Jim Fox. Miller, 78, retired after 43 years in the Kings' broadcast booth on March 2, 2017. Although his legacy is planted in Southern California, he also is notable in Las Vegas' hockey history by helping to introduce NHL hockey to this city.

For the first time in NHL history, during a game, Kings goaltender Kelly Hrudey wore a helmet camera. He recalled the experience during a 1997 interview with Dan Marrazza and VegasGoldenKnights.com.

"I remember so much about that game," Hrudey recalled. "Of course, when the game started, it was like just a normal hockey game — other than being outdoors in the desert in September."

Back then, Kings broadcasts were on Prime Ticket, and the helmet cam idea was theirs.

"Somebody in their production team came up with the idea and approached me well in advance of the game," Hrudey recalled. "The moment the question was asked of me of whether I'd wear a helmet-mounted camera and microphone, I was all for it. I think we had a couple of dry runs of how it would work with my equipment and the things I would experience from that standpoint."

The camera was a bit cumbersome.

"The camera itself was not an issue," he said. "It may have been for part of warmups. Even after the game, I remember thinking that it wasn't so bad. The camera mounted on my helmet was no problem whatsoever. The only thing that was a concern of mine was the battery pack and the size of it. I was a guy who was a heavy sweater. The last thing I needed was a warm, wet battery pack strapped to my back and pants."

Hrudey went on to add, "Being in 1991, the battery

pack and the camera itself were enormous. I can't recall exactly how much it weighed. The battery was taped to the back of my pants with all sorts of duct tape to ensure that this large battery pack wasn't going to come loose during the game. It might not look as though a goaltender is all that busy. But trust me, there are a lot of movements and you're soaking wet, and all these things came into play that might allow this battery pack to come free."

In an interview in 2023, Hrudey recalled that Hrudey Cam microphone malfunctioned. "The mic didn't work the entire time," he recalled. "Despite that, I told them I enjoyed doing it."

Hrudey's recollection of what the game meant was monumental. In his interview 25 years past the game, Hrudey said. "When you play on a team with Wayne Gretzky, you become so much more aware of trying to grow the game. I had no problem in doing something like this. I don't know how it ever happened that I never got asked again (to wear a helmet camera). But it's too bad. I still think in today's game, with today's technology, that it would be really cool. It wouldn't be cumbersome at all for a goaltender to wear a camera on his head. It would be amazing footage with HD capabilities."

Prime Ticket, which no longer exists, rebroadcast the game dozens of times. Even now, the NHL and MSG Network run the tape from time to time.

"The people at Prime Ticket were so grateful that they gave me a bottle of Cristal champagne — a treat was something I had never had before," Hrudey said before a broadcast of a Calgary Flames game in 2023.

Not So Grand Entrance

For the players, it was a long walk from the hotel to the rink. The entrance for the players was not so grand as they had to change in the casino, quite a trek from the rink. Players recalled the long trudge from the casino in the interview 25 years later by Marrazza.

Bernie Nicholls of the Rangers: "Probably the coolest thing was, I think we dressed in Caesars Palace. We had to go through the casino. You threw your equipment on, and whenever yoVIPs

u're coming through a casino, there's everything there. Slot machines, card dealers. I remember there was a long walk out to the rink. Walking out with the skyline and all the big buildings there, just looking up and being outside in Las Vegas. The view was spectacular. Second to none."

Luc Robitaille: "Yeah, it was a long walk over from Caesars."

Hrudey: "It was a unique thing because I recall walking over to the game through the dressing room

we had with John Vanbiesbrouck. He was starting for the Rangers. Never in my life had I walked to the rink with the opposing goaltender."

Drop The Puck

The air temperature at the puck drop was around 85 °F (29 °C), going as high as 95 °F (35 °C) during the course of the game, with 28% humidity. There was no official attendance reported as many guests were complementary VIPs. Estimates ranged from 13,000 to more than 16,000 fans. The Kings were captained by Gretzky, while the Rangers had yet to name a captain for the season. The game was officiated by referee Rob Shick, with linesmen Mike Cvik and Shane Heyer.

The game was also historic in that it featured the first appearance of the new Wayne Gretzky-Jari Kurri-Tomas Sandstrom line.

The Rangers started the game well, with goals by Tony Amonte and Doug Weight for a 2-0 lead at the end of the first period.

"We fell behind 2-0 and I was getting heckled," Hrudey said before broadcasting his Flames game in 2023. "The fans were really giving it to me. I thought it was a little bit harsh. They (New York fans) hated me from when I played for the Islanders. I knew that I could be lousy no more."

In the second period, the Kings countered with goals by Tony Granato, Brian Benning and Sylvain Couturier to take a 3−2 lead.

"There was a really great atmosphere," Hrudey said. "That's what I remember most. It was extremely competitive. Hrudey allowed only the two opening goals wearing the 'Hrudey Cam' and was Las Vegas' first winning goalie.

You're Bugging Me!!!

The last period was anything but typical.

"We said for the last seven minutes we said nobody could hit anybody, so there was no hitting the last seven minutes," Gretzky told the national TV audience during the 2023 Cup Finals.

The Kings added two more goals in the third period by Jari Kurri and Gretzky for a 5−2 win.

The Great One's goal was certainly memorable and should have capped off a memorable evening, but what will be remembered most was an invasion of jumping crickets/grasshoppers that blanketed the ice.

When the grasshoppers appeared still is under contention. There may have been a few that found their way toward the end of the second period, but the invasion was in full force in the third.

Gretzky thought it was the ice they were after.

"By the end of the game, they had these bugs that

A Memorable Night in NHL History at Caesars Palace

IN THE 75 YEARS OF THE NHL, never has there been a stranger night. The air temperature at puck drop was around 85 °F (29 °C), going as high as 95 °F (35 °C) during the game, with 28% humidity. The ice held up throughout, despite the siege of insects. The Rangers started the game goals by Tony Amonte and Doug Weight for a 2−0 lead at the end of the first. In the second, the Kings answered with goals by Tony Granato, Brian Benning and Sylvain Couturier to take a 3−2 lead. The Kings added two goals in the third period by Jari Kurri and Wayne Gretzky for a 5−2 win in front of a packed house.

were flying into the ice thinking it was water," The Great One said on TNT.

In the postgame press conference, Gretzky admitted he tripped when he hit a grasshopper. He said, "Look, I've ice skated since I was four years old and I thought I had seen everything until tonight."

While certainly unusual (and perhaps a bit unsettling), scientists claim that this particular species of grasshopper was completely harmless. The common species of pallid-winged grasshoppers were native to the deserts of western North America and were just following their typical migration patterns after wet winters or springs.

Twenty-five years later, the memories were vivid for both sides in their recall 25 years after the event on GoldenKniights.com.

Robitaille: On the funny side, what none of us can forget is the bugs. Those big grasshoppers were jumping on the white ice because it was so bright.

Hrudey: I'm sure those grasshoppers and those locusts had never experienced ice in their lives. I'm sure they were pretty confused about what was going on. They were probably thinking: 'Who are these guys playing hockey, and what are they doing in our parking lot?'

Robitaille: By the end of the period, it seemed like there were 100 of them on the ice. Probably an inch or two inches long. These suckers were big. It seemed like they were flying in, would jump a couple times and then just freeze.

Hrudey: They weren't crawling. But there's no question that, on occasion, they would be propelled toward you. I don't recall actually getting hit in the face. But there were some casualties amongst the locusts that night. Then they started coming in swarms.

Bernie Nicholls: It's tough enough going against hockey players. But when you've got to fight some bugs when you're skating down the ice, that's annoying. But it didn't take away from the atmosphere.

Hrudey was slightly perturbed when the grasshoppers came in his recall in 2023. "All of us were freaked out about it. It was really gross. I'm not going to lie and say three inches, but I had to sweep my crease clear every once in a while."

Basically, the swarm is a natural phenomenon. Swarms of this type of grasshopper or an offshoot locust often appear in the desert out of nowhere and sometimes stay for prolonged periods of time. An invasion occurred in Elko in 2023 and created quite a stinky health hazard over an extended period.

The ice surface that caused panic earlier in the day wasn't an issue.

Robitaille said, "I don't think the ice was that bad. It was pretty good. In those days, when we played games in Miami and Tampa Bay, the ice was way worse. We were pleased with the quality of the ice. It wasn't the way it was in Edmonton, but it was playable."

An exhibition with the Boston Bruins and New York Islanders scheduled for the Florida Suncoast Dome on Friday was canceled after workers tried unsuccessfully for an hour to make the ice playable.

Bob May's crew saved the event.

"They were all part of hockey history," Rich Rose said. "It was something no one had done. I mean, I'm sure virtually everybody who played that night skated outdoors when they were young, but never thinking that they would do it on the Major League level. For the backdrop of this game, we had good ice and a sellout crowd."

"It was a knowledgeable community," Hrudey said of the fans. "Not the savvy of Toronto or Montreal, but people here knew the game."

"For me, preseason was extremely important," he added, "It was the last preseason game for me. I needed to play well before the season, and my teammates were the same way. The fans got their money's worth on that. I didn't know what to expect and didn't know it would be that big of a game."

When asked if the game brought the Kings closer together as a team, Hrudey said, "It's funny you say that. It did to a certain degree. The attitude we had after that game brought us together early. The game and the flights forced us to get to know each other. Not one guy had a complaint about the event. Everything about it was a magical hockey game. I had a lot of great memories from it."

After the game, Hrudey admitted having a few beers. He also was signed prior to the season to a four-year, $2.65-million contract. Hrudey made $575,000 that season, then $650,000, $700,000, and $725,000 in the option year. That showed the difference between the Gretzky paycheck and his teammates. Two members of the Kings who played in the game, Rob Blake and Robitaille, went on to become management in the Kings organization.

"Caesars had the reputation of putting on the biggest of events," sportswriter Steve Carp said. "And Rich Rose was tireless in his pursuit of pulling this one off."

"This game gave me the opportunity to put on one of my great sports accomplishments," Rose said. "The Kings-Rangers game is somewhat of an ultimate achievement.

"All in all, such a great experience," Rose said. "It was fun just to do it and see our people put it on and see how much the people enjoyed it. We were able to say we did something no one else had ever done. How many times do you get to do that?"

"They didn't have that much in attendance," Rose recalled. "We pulled our game off in grand style. But if it wasn't for Bruce in the background and Wayne as the main draw, it never would have been so historic. I've dealt with athletes in virtually every sport, and the players were genuinely excited to be there. They are a big part of hockey history in Las Vegas."

We had Wayne Gretzky playing in Vegas; it was just awesome!" morning DJ Mike O'Brian said. "But in Vegas, you know what? We do what we do, right? You know, like, say, yeah, we can build a rink. We can get the Kings and Gretzky here. We can get the Rangers here. We could do

that. How hard can that be? And Caesars and the Kings just did it. After the event, I'm sure everybody was thinking, yes, hockey could work here. Hockey could actually work here! It took decades to get it here, but nonetheless, I would like to think that game had something to do with bringing NHL hockey to Vegas along with the minor levels. It was exciting. It was. And now you see what we have here."

Gretzky saw it coming days before the game.

"I still remember the morning I had breakfast with Gretzky and his wife, and he said, 'You guys were way out in front and ahead of your time,'" Cooper said.

He reiterated that on TNT during the Cup finals.

"We had 15,000 people at the game, and people loved it," Gretzky said. "Right then and there, we knew Vegas was going to be a great hockey city."

Growth Spurt Begins

The Amateur Skate and the outdoor game also gave a shot in the arm to amateur hockey for both kids and adults at the Santa Fe, where former juniors and college players gathered to scrimmage for fun.

"A few weeks after the Caesars game, the owner of Kilroys rented the Santa Fe ice for a couple hours on Friday mornings, and former junior and college players came out, some of them from California, including Pat Brisson," Gubbe said.

Brisson is now a National Hockey League Players Association (NHLPA) agent with Creative Artists Agency. He is also the father of Brendan Brisson, a Vegas Golden Knights first-round draft pick. Brisson has represented Jack Hughes, Sidney Crosby, Patrick Kane, Anže Kopitar and Jonathan Toews.

"They used to have to have four goalies on Fridays because they didn't believe in defense," Gubbe said. "It was all just skating up and down and shooting, and they wore the goalies out, including me, with all the rubber we saw."

Leagues at Santa Fe started to fill up, although the hockey played in those leagues was lacking skill. Entry into pro hockey leagues followed soon thereafter.

Chapter 5
Aces Up

In 1992. The Las Vegas Aces became the first "true professional" hockey team in Las Vegas.

Wayne Gretzky may have been the first to predict hockey would blossom here, but then the real work had to begin. Fans had to be cultivated and youth hockey had to spawn. The first to be considered true professionals were the Las Vegas Aces, who became the first team to pay its players and the first organization to develop a youth league.

"True Ice Hockey Professional" means the primary occupation of the players is ice hockey, 24/7.

By definition, the Las Vegas Aces hockey team, not the Women's Basketball team that now wears the name, undoubtedly became the start of professional hockey as a team sport in Las Vegas. The Aces were put together by a group of local hockey players who had been organizing games wherever there was a sheet of ice large enough to accommodate them.

Hockey was huge nationwide but was still in its infancy in the City of Lights at all levels. There was no organized youth hockey due to the lack of a facility capable of handling the volume of kids interested in learning, with few willing to teach them.

Due to the transient nature of Las Vegas during the boom years of the late '80s and early '90s, hundreds of thousands of people migrated from the Midwest and the East Coast, and along with them came the equipment to play the sports they cherished.

With the Ice Palace no longer in business, there were no facilities to play at due to the simple fact Las Vegas is in the middle of a desert. The complexity of maintaining an ice rink in an adverse and elevated climate year-round was thought to be impractical. The risks and expenses were huge for a city where 99% of the ice is served in glasses or used to chill buffets. For any sheet of ice to support amateur and professional ice-related programs, unusual challenges had to be conquered, not to mention a cost factor of 2 to 3 times that of a similar facility in a cooler climate.

The Santa Fe

Never had Las Vegas seen anything that even resembled a professional ice arena, let alone one that could seat more than 2,000 fans. It wasn't until 1991 that Sahara Gaming and the Paul and Sue Lowden family decided to take the risk and build a casino resort that included the first professional ice arena capable of handling both hockey and figure skating, amateur and professional.

With the ice arena built to accommodate all forms of organized and open skating, Las Vegas could be serious about ice hockey on all levels.

Anyone can build an ice arena, but "If you build it, they may not come," specifically in the middle of the desert. Anywhere else in the country, and particularly in the Midwest and Northeast, every sheet of ice was booked solid. This included amateur programs, both youth and senior, professional teams, and a variety of leagues, sometimes on waiting lists for ice to be open. And whatever ice the hockey players left open became swallowed up immediately by the figure skaters.

Youth programs had a mere spattering of skaters from other states now living in Vegas, and the senior-level teams were predominantly ex-collegiate, but certainly, no players who would be identified as professional. All of them had other income sources and did not consider themselves "full-time" athletes compensated by hockey.

It was not until 1992 that an avid hockey player and a huge fan of hockey, Maurice Slepica (living in Vegas at the time), decided he would try and organize a team of senior players that could be competitive professionally. Slepica was able to convince some Senior A & B level teams to come to Vegas and play them on weekends. With the support of the Santa Fe Hotel and Casino, he was able to provide incentives such as rooms and buffet discounts to attract USA hockey amateur senior level and club teams to play on weekends. The Santa Fe team was called the "Las Vegas Aces," and the 1992-1993 hockey season was hailed as the first organized semi-pro hockey team to play in Vegas.

The Aces played as many games as possible in the 1992-1993 season. They did create enough fan support to attract attention and start sports enthusiasts to wonder if professional hockey might have a chance in Vegas.

While Slepica did well in launching the Aces, he also began to organize youth hockey at the Santa Fe. However, his career path and personal interests were elsewhere, so a search was on for someone to step in and take his accomplishments to the next level, and that someone was Robert (Bob) Lawson from Michigan.

Lawson's parents lived in Las Vegas, and they befriended both the Lowdens as well as Slepica. The conversation of son Robert and his professional sports career had been discussed often. Lawson also was a lifelong hockey player and coach and even spent some time in officials stripes while also owning a successful sports management company, Lawson Associates.

LAS VEGAS
ACES
H O C K E Y

1 9 9 3 - 1 9 9 4
ACTION
SOUVENIR PROGRAM

In addition to his sports management company, Lawson was a successful entrepreneur, owning several manufacturing companies in the machine and cutting tool industries. In 1993, he was introduced to Slepica, and an immediate friendship occurred.

Slepica was ready to make a change and head back to the upper Midwest, and Lawson took the reins in May of 1993 at the Santa Fe Ice Arena as the Hockey Director, which included the Aces and youth programs.

"I felt he was absolutely right for the job," Slepica said.

Lawson Arrived in May 1993

"It's one thing to step into a situation that's similar to this anywhere in the country and become a success with the proper skills and attributes," Lawson said, "But you must remember that as far as the majority of true Vegas locals were concerned, ice was for drinks, a Zamboni sounded like an Italian food, and a who the hell knew what a "Puck" was used for. The challenge of putting the team together was the easy part as Maurice had done a pretty decent job of identifying the available talent and organizing them to play games, but putting an entire season together meant commitment from these players, and that's where it got very difficult."

In the early '90s, Vegas was exploding in remarkable growth. The number of transients coming and going to the city meant a variety of shift options for work. Also, there were only a couple of professional hockey leagues the Aces could take part in, and they were up and down the West Coast, including Alaska.

"We had slowly put together a team, we had an amazing facility, and we had owners who definitely had an interest in having a professional team. We also had adults from far and wide who were interested in their son learning how to play hockey and having an organization to play in," Lawson said. "My assignment was to get the youth hockey program growing with a solid organization already in place."

The Southern Nevada Minor Hockey Association was born out of the Santa Fe Arena.

"The key to any successful youth sports program lies within the parents and these parents were the best," Lawson said. "Of course, it helped that I was a youthful 37 years old, and I spent the last 35 involved with one of the best youth programs in the U.S., the GFHA (Greater Flint Hockey Association in Michigan), headed up by my pseudo-father Gale Cronk. There was none better, and Gale was my right hand whenever I needed any help in Vegas. We simply followed the GFHA program to the letter, including all the logistics necessary to expedite its formation and have a full-blown program in the 1993-1994 season. Hats off to Dale Lewis, President of the SNMHA."

Playing for Real

Transitioning from playing pickup games for buffet tickets to competing in a full league schedule with travel costs and overnight stays presented a significant challenge for the Las Vegas Aces. As the team's General Manager and Head Coach, Lawson recognized the need to elevate the team's commitment and professionalism to meet the demands of a competitive league.

To address this challenge, Lawson put together a comprehensive budget that accounted for various expenses associated with participating in a league. This included travel costs, accommodation for overnight stays during away games, and the 24/7 commitment required from the players. Presenting this budget to the team's owners was an essential step in securing the necessary financial resources to support the team's operations.

While the Aces were previously playing as a house team against various opponents, the goal now was to compete in a more structured and organized manner.

"This meant establishing a higher level of commitment from the players, both on and off the ice," Lawson said. "It required them to prioritize their hockey responsibilities and make the necessary sacrifices to compete at a professional level."

By presenting a comprehensive budget and outlining the demands and expectations of competing in a full league schedule, Lawson aimed to demonstrate the seriousness and professionalism of the Las Vegas Aces.

"It was time to sit down with the Lowdens and discuss the options," Lawson said. "But first, I knew I had to do my homework, think out of the box, and most importantly, present the budgets."

Professional sports at any level are expensive, especially when you are looking at joining a league where the closest team is a 6-hour bus ride.

It was time to "Think Outside the Box."

Positives
A. To have the basis of a solid competitive team made up of ex-collegiate and semi-pro players.
B. To have an arena that seats around 2,000 attached to a casino resort.
C. To have the support of hockey-passionate owners.

Negatives
A. Players all have other jobs.
B. The team is literally new and unknown to the Vegas community.
C. A limited budget.
D. Questionable fan support.

"I remember going through the list over and over, thinking through possible options," Lawson said. "All of a sudden, a two-by-four hit me. There are more semi-pro teams in the U.S. than imaginable, and they all have one thing in common: they love to play hockey, and they are all doing it for the passion and certainly not the money. Additionally, they also love to have fun, and what city in America can you have more fun in than Las Vegas? I thought, suppose I send out invitations to some of the best semi-pro teams from around the country for a "Weekend of Competition" against the Aces? We would include free rooms, meals, and ALL drinks for the entire weekend. The idea was to bring these teams in from a variety of cities that would also draw a fan base from the locals in Las Vegas who hailed from Philly, Detroit, St. Paul, Chicago, Duluth, Long Island, and on and on. Within days, I had teams on waiting lists. Before you knew it, we had every Friday and Saturday evening booked from October through March."

Zero costs to the Aces, and with each weekend a different city, the casino was attracting a new customer base made up of sports fans, many of them gamblers. The win/win for all allowed Lawson to put together a pay rate for the players, along with several other perks such as available (and flexible around the weekend) second jobs for them as well.

The little-known Aces started selling out the arena, and by mid-season, it was difficult to get a seat. It was impossible for the community to ignore what was going on at the Santa Fe arena.

From 1993 to 1995, the Aces needed teams to play from the first professional hockey league on the West Coast. These teams created the base for the PSHL, which basically revolved around these teams until 2003. Teams that played a full schedule with the Las Vegas Aces in the 1993-1994 season were. Alaska (ACES), Bakersfield (FOG), Fresno (FALCONS), Las Vegas (ACES), San Diego (GULLS),

In 2003, the West Coast Hockey League ceased operations. The ECHL board of governors approved

Myron Freund dished out some big hits for the Aces.

membership applications from the Anchorage/Alaska Aces, the Bakersfield Condors, the Fresno Falcons, the Idaho Steelheads, the Las Vegas Wranglers, the Long Beach Ice Dogs and the San Diego Gulls, as well as from potential teams in Ontario, California, and Reno, Nevada.

Myron Freund and wife Patti with the Hanson Brothers.

Aces Throw a Challenge

From the very beginning, Lawson treated the Las Vegas Aces as an NHL team, and the press and promotional efforts reflected that perception as the Aces became entrenched in the community.

"Surprisingly, many members of the press didn't distinguish between the Aces and the IHL Las Vegas Thunder,' he said. "This created a lot of confusion, which was part of my strategy. The primary goal was to generate buzz and excitement around the Aces, and it worked, as they garnered just as much attention as the Thunder in the early stages. The Aces were constantly in the news, and the media coverage contributed to our growing popularity."

Despite the confusion, the Aces consistently sold out their games every weekend, indicating dedicated support from the local community. However, this didn't take away from the Thunder, who had notable players and a significant budget.

A compelling subplot emerged as Lawson challenged Bob Strumm, the GM of the Thunder, to a game between the two teams. Lawson recognized an opportunity to further establish the credibility of the Aces and highlight the value of attending their games compared to the higher-priced Thunder games.

Strumm was unlikely to consider taking on Lawson's Aces due to logistical constraints, IHL regulations, and the potential liability associated with their preferred players. Lawson, on the other hand, had assembled a talented and tough group of players who were known for their style of play referred to as "Bush League Hockey."

This style of play was characterized by its vigorous adherence to the rules, aggression, and rugged competitiveness, embodying the essence of the sport's early

days. The Aces, with their tough and skilled players boasting backgrounds in junior, collegiate and professional hockey, become the epitome of this definition.

The media seized the hype and published articles in local papers, while local sports personalities pitched the challenge on various TV programs. However, the game between the two teams never materializes due to the lose-lose scenario it presented for the Thunder.

There have been many arguments regarding the "First Real Professional Hockey Team in Las Vegas being the Thunder, but just as many will argue, the Aces were the inaugural true professional team to compete on ice. After all, they actually started one year earlier under Slepica.

In support of that argument for the Aces, it doesn't take much other than a list of the roster of the Aces to see the team was more than a house team of beer-drinking guys playing pick-up games.

The support received through major sponsorships further reinforced the pro status of the Aces. In the 1993-1994 season, Lawson was able to attract premier sponsors from various industries in Las Vegas. They included sponsorships from gaming establishments like the Sahara, as well as partnerships with beer and soda companies, retail outlets and automotive businesses. These sponsors recognized the opportunity to be associated with professional hockey and invested cash money.

Weekend games allowed fans to enjoy the action without worrying about late nights or school nights. It also catered to couples looking for a sports entertainment option, as they could attend a game and then continue their evening within the casino complex. The Aces offered a wide range of promotional packages that went beyond standard tickets and snacks, including buffet packages, overnight rooming packages, casino packages and often free beer promotions. The value and variety of these packages made the Aces hockey game an affordable entertainment value for locals.

"Those who attended the game through these packages became instant fans," Lawson said. "Not only for the perks, but also because of the high level of hockey and the toughness displayed by the Aces. The competitiveness and physicality of the team made it impossible not to want to return for more."

Within the first month of play that season, the Aces' arena, known as the "Barn," was consistently selling out, and these were purchased tickets and packages rather than comped tickets handed out as promotions by other sports teams. This made the Aces not only the first professional hockey team in Las Vegas but also the most profitable, as the Thunder was not profitable at all.

The tougher and more aggressively a team plays, the more attention they tend to receive, and often, success follows suit. The gladiator-like atmosphere of well-conditioned athletes facing off with limited physical protection, armed with sticks and chasing a hard rubber puck at high speeds, naturally leads to collisions and, at times, fights. Fans have always had an affinity for a good fight, and it energizes the crowd. Once the fight concludes, the players involved typically receive a five-minute penalty in the penalty box before returning to the game.

The Aces embodied this tough and aggressive style of play, and the player who led the pack was Myron Freund, the formidable and large playing coach. Myron, a semi-professional player from Portland, Oregon, showcased an unmatched level of determination, commitment and toughness every time he stepped on the ice. He played in every professional game for the Aces, regardless of injury or physical adversity.

One notable incident exemplifying his resilience occurred during a fight with an opponent, where the opposing player gouged Myron's eye out of its socket. Despite this horrific injury, Myron did not miss the next game, having his eye popped back into its socket to continue competing.

Another example of Myron's dedication came during the final playoffs of the 1993-1994 season when he was needed on the team but had an arm cast. He made the bold decision to cut off his own cast, sacrificing personal comfort for the benefit of the team.

The Daniels Brothers Arrive

Lawson and his marketing manager, Richard Gubbe, knew the town and its people well and also knew they had to not only deliver a solid competitive team on the ice, but the game also had to be an event, and above all else, leaving the fans wanting more.

It's one thing for any team, in any market, in any sport, to have an opening show with a fancy mascot, but the true test is making the fans as excited at the end of the game as well as the beginning.

By mid-season 1993-1994, between the marketing efforts of the Aces as well as the Thunder, Las Vegans knew what hockey was and also were coming to both arenas to make their own comparisons. Some liked the European style of the Thunder, some the physicality and toughness of the Aces.

This was so obvious to Lawson that he and Gubbe decided to kick it up a notch. With the efforts of Randy Huartson, Aces head scout, the target became the Daniels, three full-blooded Mistawasis First Nation aboriginal, you got it, all Cree Indians. All were born and raised in Prince Albert, Saskatchewan, Canada.

"You would be hard-pressed to find this much hockey talent within one family, let alone the success of 4 brothers all making it to the professional level, including the NHL for 2 of them," Lawson said. "Along with hockey skills, the brothers all had the same style of play, and that was being the toughest and most determined (to use the term loosely) on the ice every second they were on it."

"If you're a hockey fan, which I assume you are if you're reading this, you have watched "Slap Shot" more than once, and the favored players are the Hanson's," Lawson said. "The Daniels make the Hanson's look like a midget team when it comes to style of play. Bottom line is that all four, and specifically the three, Mark, Scott, Gary, were just what was needed to win the fan attraction battle in Las Vegas."

From the first puck drop until the closing minutes, the Daniels did whatever was expected of them on the ice (and sometimes off as well.), and during the 1990s, hockey, in general, coined a term for a class of player called "policemen" and that's what the Daniels were — all four of them.

"It was never finesse, or stick handling, or skating prowess that impressed the scouts looking at the Daniels," Lawson said, "Without question, it was how strong they checked, how aggressive they were, and how well they could throw a punch when needed. In a town built upon the primary sport being boxing, the Daniels tied the two sports together. The locals may not have known the rules very well, but they understood a good right or left hand."

"The Daniels were an immediate fan favorite as expected from the first minute they hit the ice," Gubbe said. "They became local celebrities of sorts."

The fans reacted with their pockets, and the arena began to be sold out weeks in advance. Merchandising followed, and the marketing of the Aces and the Daniels brothers was everywhere.

"Parades, autograph appearances, school promotions, event appearances, TV interviews and more," Lawson said. "The Aces may have been playing in a lesser league to the Thunder, but the Las Vegas locals didn't care, especially when you got all of the above, and a family of four was half the price of the Thunder ticket."

Keeping the Fan Base

During the 1993-1994 season, with two professional hockey teams competing in Las Vegas, the battle to attract paying fans through sponsorship dollars became a challenge. The Thunder, backed by the Stickney family and the successful Las Vegas Stars baseball team, seemed poised to secure major sponsorship money easily. Caesars Palace backed both teams, for instance. On the other hand, the Lowden family name, one of the largest casino families in Las Vegas through Sahara Gaming, was the Aces' main backer.

Major beer distributors, for example, had to decide where to allocate their sports sponsorship budgets. Should they invest in a new and unproven IHL hockey team with an entirely out-of-state roster, or should the money go to another professional hockey team with a year of experience owned by one of their significant casino accounts? Lawson recognized the opportunity to capitalize on this situation and treated the Aces as though they were an NHL team.

One of the first steps taken was assembling a front office composed of local talent who were already familiar with the Las Vegas community. Crucially, a media marketing expert was brought in to create hype and ensure that the Las Vegas Aces' name, brand, and players were constantly in front of the locals. Lawson connected with Gubbe, the editor of Las Vegas Magazine and an independent sportswriter and PR consultant. Their immediate friendship, fueled by their shared passion for hockey, led to the co-authoring of this book three decades later.

Lawson and Gubbe launched an extensive marketing campaign. This included ticket promotions,

Aces goalie Eric Danielson.

scheduling interviews on major local sports shows, print media, advertising, and promotional events that had the players hitting the streets for the next season. By the start of the Aces' second season at the Santa Fe Arena, one-third of the arena had been sold to season ticket holders. Once the season began, the Aces consistently sold out every night, often to standing-room-only crowds. Professional hockey had firmly taken root.

The phrase "Vegas professional hockey happened in Vegas and stayed in Vegas" encapsulates the success and impact of the Aces' arrival and the strong connection they forged. In the middle of the season, it became apparent to the Vegas community that hockey was truly a new sport with enormous potential.

"Why would any tourist from the Midwest or East Coast want to fly 2,000 miles or more from the cold and ice to go to a hockey game in Las Vegas, especially since the average stay was 3 to 4 days?" Lawson said. "It became very prevalent there needed to be mostly locals as the fan base."

The major beer and soda sponsors were faced with splitting the monies with the Thunder or risk business with Sahara Gaming and their four major properties in Las Vegas.

Ticket promotions for the Aces were focused on the locals, with family packages as well as couples that included buffet comps and hotel comps, all tied into the purchase of an Aces ticket package, hence the sold-out crowds and an ever-increasing fan base.

With this ever-increasing fan base on both ends of Las Vegas came the inevitable curiosity of the fans to the comparisons of the Aces vs the Thunder.

"As the season progressed, and the Aces kept winning, who could ask for a better building block for Hockey in Las Vegas," Lawson quipped.

"I found it interesting that when the Knights took to the ice in 2017, ownership of the Golden Knights chose Gerard Gallant to coach the team," Lawson said. "Gallant was infamous for the exact type of toughness on the ice that the Aces introduced to Las Vegas 24 years prior."

That toughness became a trademark of the Golden Knights and was particularly prevalent in the team's Stanley Cup-winning season.

The 1993-1994 Las Vegas Aces team. **Back Row:** Chad Olsen, Kevin O'Connor, Andre Sioui, Gary Daniels, Billy Grum, Howie Thomas, Mark Daniels, Marty Raymond, Michael Laughlin, Steve McGrath, Terry Doyle, Kevin Kamenski, Dave Hernesman. **Front Row:** Gordon Lawes, Travis Schaeffer, Joe DiGiacomo, Frank Salgado – Trainer, Bob Lawson GM/Head Coach, Karen Doherty, Ice Rink Mgr., Myron Freund – Player/Coach, Randy Huartson – Asst. Coach, Donny Holmstrom, Bobby Pezzulo, Eric Danielson.
Not pictured: Dan Green. Karen Doherty was responsible from bringing over Russian skater Victor Petrenko and training him for the Olympics at the Santa Fe.

Aces players Donny Holmstrom and Kevin Kamenski face off in road and home jerseys Taken at Santa Fe for the 1993-1994 season. The blue jersey was the primary jersey for home games.

Chapter 6
Star Power and the Las Vegas Thunder

The franchise that amplified the NHL's future in Las Vegas was the Las Vegas Thunder. Getting an IHL franchise was a big deal for the city, and the team quickly was embraced. The Thunder built a fan base that showed hockey could make it long-term in the desert over six years, despite poor management. The Thunder's tumultuous tenure that began in 1993 had more ups and downs than a flopping goalie before exiting six years later.

The Thomas & Mack Center, an arm of the University of Nevada, Las Vegas, had the ability to put up temporary NHL-sized ice and the Thunder had their own boards. With some renovations, the largest venue in town would serve as a site for the city's first big-time team.

The T&M was under the management of longtime Vegas entertainment kingpin Pat Christensen. He and booking chief Darren Libonati decided to shop around for a hockey team beginning in 1992. They believed the outdoor game at Caesars showed there was interest enough to support a season of games.

A graduate of the University of Wisconsin in Madison where he won an NCAA wrestling national championship at 167 pounds as a senior in 1976, Christenson carved out an impressive career in Las Vegas in venue development, event programming and sponsorships.

Christenson moved to Las Vegas in 1980 to be an assistant wrestling coach at UNLV. In 1983, he was promoted to assistant director of the newly built 18,500-seat Thomas & Mack Center, which was unfinished and projected to be a cash drain on UNLV. At the same time, UNLV also took over management of the 30,000-seat Las Vegas Silver Bowl, then called Sam Boyd Stadium.

Christenson was tasked with developing programming and overseeing operations for both venues. From 1983 to 1992, the Thomas & Mack Center and the Silver Bowl were arguably the two most successful collegiate venues in the state. Christenson booked every event they could that toured the country, averaging 175 events per year in both venues. By 1990, both venues were solvent and had completed $15 million worth of improvements, amassing a sizeable

cash reserve.

In 1991, Christenson was promoted to director of both venues. He lobbied for and managed a $40 million renovation of both sites. After all his accomplishments, he was named Las Vegas' "Most Influential Sports Figure" by the Las Vegas Sun in 2007 and recently retired.

Best 2 Out of 3 Falls

In late 1992, Christenson and Libonati began shopping for a upper-echelon minor league pro hockey team. They drew interest from the Stickney family, father Hank, and son Ken from California, known for being profitable minor league baseball team owners, including the Las Vegas Stars.

Hank and his son also were investors in California minor league baseball affiliates, Hank owning the San Bernardino Spirit, Ken, the Palm Springs Angels.

"The Stickneys believed themselves to be strong negotiators," Libonati recalled in a 2023 interview. "What they failed to realize was that we were strong negotiators and Las Vegas was the world we grew up in."

Libonati had a strong background negotiating contracts for entertainment shows, boxing events and concerts. He and Christenson agreed to meet the Stickneys on their home turf in Ontario, Calif. They arrived after crunching numbers and putting together a strong offer to give the Stickneys.

"On the flight down to Ontario, we had a strategy that this is the number that we will accept as an all-in flat fee for each game," Libonati said. "When we got there, they wanted half that number."

After being floored by the counteroffer, signing the Stickneys, who had a name and logo ready to go, seemed in jeopardy. Christensen and Libonati had a code worked out that if Libonati would close this notebook forcefully, they would stand up and leave. And sure enough....

"No one says we needed the Thunder," Libonati said. "We would like to have hockey and be a wonderful partner, but we don't NEED hockey. We are really successful as a venue operation. Having hockey was going to be a bigger headache than anything."

The Stickneys drew the ire of Christensen after a couple of choice insults.

"They were dealing with an all-American wrestler in Pat Christensen," Libonati said. "Pat said why don't we get on the floor, and the best two out of three falls gets the deal they want. He was half-heartedly joking and half serious."

After a back and forth, the Vegas contingent was ready to leave. Then tensions grew.

"It didn't take very long and they made some comments to Pat that we were being cowards," Libonati said. "That seemed to be the negotiating style the Stickneys had."

Then came Libonati closing his notebook with aggression.

"We got up to leave rather than get into an argument," he said. "We got up and said we were done. They said we were weak. We walked down the hallway into the lobby. We both said we saw this coming. We said, 'Let's just get on a plane and go home. We're not standing for this nonsense. We know who we are.'"

Then came a sudden change of heart.

"Mr. Stickney comes running down the hall and said 'come back, come back,'" Libonati said. "He (Ken) said, 'We're sorry. This is no way to start a relationship.' We ended back in the room, and we stayed with the numbers I had projected."

For the next five years plus.

"It was all good until it wasn't," Libonati said with the future in mind.

In 1993, Christensen received the money from the board at UNLV to expand the Thomas & Mack Center to accommodate the needs of a growing national rodeo and a tunnel to accommodate the Thunder's need for a larger opening. Concrete had to be removed in the end zone so the rink could be expanded, and a larger tunnel was needed for the Zamboni machine.

"We had some upfront costs we had to incur to make this thing work," Libonati said. "We retrofitted the arena and pushed back some concrete to make the room

Bob Strumm

they needed to make it work. The Thunder even paid for some of it."

Libonati soon left the T&M with former UNLV Athletic Director Dennis Finfrock to open the MGM Grand Garden Arena, which also had the capability to make ice. Soon after arriving at the MGM, the two met with officials of the Los Angeles Kings and would later start the Frozen Fury series with the Los Angeles Kings playing a variety of teams during one exhibition game and later, the Golden Knights were playing an exhibition game there yearly.

All Things Stallworth

Steve Stallworth is all things sports in Las Vegas. Stallworth has had a distinguished career in Las Vegas, first on the gridiron, then he carved out a lasting impression at the Thomas & Mack before moving on to The Orleans and the South Point in various positions. He had the Sales and Marketing job at Thomas & Mack before moving on to The Orleans with hotel/casino magnate Michael Gaughan to oversee a new hockey facility as vice president and general manager. Then he followed Gaughan as the general manager of the new South Point Arena, Equestrian Center and Priefert Pavilion. The South Point Equestrian Center Complex, which includes two additional arenas as part of the Priefert Pavilion, is widely regarded as a premier equestrian facility in the United States.

A natural leader with a down-home Arizona cowboy style, his experience also includes being the director of corporate sales for the Canadian Football League's Las Vegas Posse, director of marketing and sales for the Arena Football League's Las Vegas Sting and the Continental Indoor Soccer League's Las Vegas Dust Devils.

A 1987 UNLV graduate in Communication Studies, Stallworth played quarterback for the UNLV Rebels football team from 1982-1986. He was named team captain and received the scholar athlete award in 1985

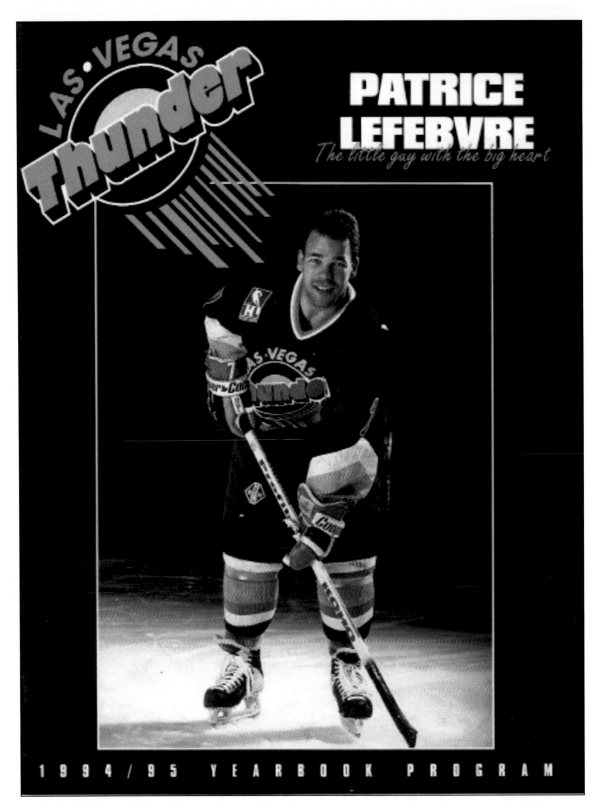

LAS·VEGAS Thunder

PATRICE LEFEBVRE
The little guy with the big heart

1 9 9 4 / 9 5 Y E A R B O O K P R O G R A M

and 1986. During his career at UNLV, Stallworth threw for 3,789 yards and 23 touchdowns.

Stallworth has served on the board of trustees for the Southern Nevada Sports Hall of Fame, the Las Vegas Bowl, the UNLV Football Foundation, the Southern Nevada Sporting Event Committee, and the Southern Nevada Conservancy. He is also a youth football coach and a former elected member of the Nevada State Board of Education.

"I was at UNLV when Pat got the money to expand the Thomas & Mack Center, which allowed us to get the tunnel for them, and the Thunder even paid for some of it," he recalled.

Then came the not-so-famous scoreboard incident.

"We never had a home video screen," Stallworth said. "When the Runnin' Rebels won the National Championship, we never had a video screen. We never had the money. In 1992, they were building the new Portland Rose Garden. We bought their old board with their CRT technology. We actually thought If we can charge each event $300, we can pay for it. We pitched it to UNLV and the board bought into the idea. But

with big-name talent after the rocky start with the management. Many thought they were crazy to have hockey in the desert, but they knew Las Vegas was ready when the puck dropped on Oct. 15, 1993, in front of a sold-out crowd.

The task of recruiting players for an expansion team is no easy feat, but the Stickneys turned to Bob Strumm, a well-respected, experienced hockey coach and scout with a knack for seizing talent, including up-and-coming players like 17-year-old Radek Bonk and 20-year-old Ruslan Salei – both later becoming top 10 overall draft picks in the NHL.

Strumm's roster turned to inaugural Head Coach Butch Goring for leadership. In their first year of existence, the Thunder had the best record in the league, winning the Huber Trophy and a division title. The Huber Trophy was awarded annually by the International League Hockey to the team with the most points during the regular season, a feat they would repeat in year three under Strumm and Head Coach Chris McSorley, whose brother Marty played in the Outdoor Game at Caesars.

The Thunder finished with 115 points and a 52-18-11 record. They topped that performance in 1995-1996 when they again finished with the league's best record (122 points, 57-17-8). The Thunder lost in the conference finals that season.

Throughout the team's history, they garnered player development deals with the Phoenix Coyotes of the NHL, the ECHL's Knoxville Cherokees and Mississippi Sea Wolves and Russian club Lokomotiv Yaroslavl.

Throughout the team's history, several notable NHL players would wear the Las Vegas Thunder jersey, including NHL stars such as Clint Malarchuk, Curtis Joseph, Petr Nedved, Alexei Yashin, Rod Buskas, Bonk and Brent Gretzky.

Yashin, the 20-year-old rising star of the NHL's Ottawa Senators, arrived in 1994. The IHL publicly discouraged its clubs from signing players under NHL contract during that league's 1994-1995 lockout. But the league didn't prevent the Stickneys from signing Yashin to a reported $200,000 one-year deal. Yashin had the right to void the contract at any time if the lockout ended. The Russian centerman tuned up the

with the Thunder, which had most of the events, we said we will split it with you. We will have one-half of the board for our sponsors, you can have one-half for your sponsors. This is a win-win. The Thunder had 42 games. We told Ken Stickney about the $300 and he said, 'No, we don't want it. You can just leave it off. We're not going to pay for it.' Our jaws almost hit the floor."

The nonprofit venue was left holding the board, so to speak.

"We were in a huge quandary," Stallworth said. "We had to hustle our asses off. We couldn't just have nothing up there. It was 10 years old at the time. We had to pay for production for each event. We had to pay cameramen and guys in the booth. We had to eat the entire cost because they wouldn't pay a dime."

The rough start just got more coarse.

"There was a lot of disharmony between us and the Stickney family all the time," Stallworth said. "Ken was the toughest."

Let's Play Ice Hockey

With the T&M ready for hockey, the Thunder made a big early splash. From the aqua uniforms and a dynamic mascot to a lush ad campaign, the initial response was felt at the turnstiles. Many who came didn't know a left-handed stick from a righty, but the International Hockey League had ties to the big league, and that was seen as a big move for Las Vegas.

The Thunder dazzled fans in the first two seasons

IHL for 15 goals and 20 assists in 24 games before the NHL re-opened for business and Yashin bailed for Ottawa.

NHL All-Star goaltender Joseph arrived the following year during a holdout with the St. Louis Blues. Like Yashin, Joseph toyed with the IHL competition (12-2-1, 1.99 GAA) for a few weeks. Then, a trade to Edmonton resolved his NHL contract woes, and he was off to the NHL.

"I was in between jobs," Joseph said. "I needed a place to play and stay sharp. Las Vegas was a good spot; they had a good team. And we had a lot of fun. Those are fond memories. I was here for about five weeks, I think."

Despite the glitzy signings and two divisional titles, the Thunder lost a reported $6 million during their first three seasons in Sin City. The IHL's business model proved to be hugely flawed. Unlike the Stickneys' minor league baseball holdings, where player costs were covered by Major League patrons, IHL teams functioned primarily as independents. Starting in 1996, the Thunder had a partial affiliation with the NHL's Phoenix Coyotes. But the Coyotes only supplied a couple of players a year. T he Stickneys were on the hook for virtually all the IHL's $1.3 million annual salary cap, plus medical and insurance costs. By the mid-1990s, it was clear that the IHL needed NHL support to survive. However IHL leaders angered the senior circuit by expanding into NHL cities like Chicago and Detroit. The NHL preferred to work with the

POWER PLAY

NOVEMBER 1993

A Look at the '93-94 IHL Rookie Crop

Nothing Matches a Shootout for Excitement

Notes and Quotes from All of Your Favorite Teams

THE OFFICIAL MAGAZINE OF THE INTERNATIONAL HOCKEY LEAGUE

more docile American Hockey League and didn't truly need the IHL.

It wasn't just the NHL names that fans clamored to see. Franchise player Patrice Lefebvre, who holds the record for all-time games played for the team, had a formidable fan base along with many other long-time team members Joe Day, Darcy Loewen, Ken Quinney, Jeff Sharples, Rhett Trombley, and the first female professional hockey player, goaltender Manon Rhéaume, to name a few. Many remained in Las Vegas following their playing days. Lefebvre brought out female fans and Bonk became a formidable player in the NHL. The local and national media gave Bonk lots of publicity.

Padded Seats

Caesars Palace had never sponsored a sports team outside of the Las Vegas Stars baseball team. Don Logan of the Stars and Thunder and Phil Cooper of Caesars built a friendship over the years, and when the Thunder arrived, Cooper did something he had never done before with a paid team sponsorship.

"I wanted to own something locally," Cooper said. "The Caesars brand was marketed nationally and internationally and not locally except for the Stars. We were never interested in any team before that. Before that, we had only bought the scoreboard for the Stars."

The deal was an out-of-the-box agreement as only Caesars would be able to dictate. Cooper had the autonomy to do darn near anything he wanted because Caesars was tops in live events, even though this was off property.

"I just wanted to have a presence that was all encompassing," Cooper said. "I did it so no one else could crash into that."

Radek Bonk Signed puck.

To make a splash, Cooper bought the advertising on the Zamboni and gave Caesar himself the keys to drive it.

"We were all over the ice, the dasher boards, patches on the jerseys, in-game announcements," Cooper said, "But the Zamboni made the biggest impact both with the crowd and the media."

Cooper made an unusual deal of getting seats for his advertising dollars as well as the signage. He knew locals wouldn't head to the Strip after the game, but the employees enjoyed the 1,200 free seats to every game.

"My relationship came from the Stars and Don Logan," Cooper said. "If it was going to be Caesars, it had to be creative, and we rode the Zamboni to some great exposure, and no one else ever did that. We used one of our Caesars to do it. I'll take the credit for that one. Did it drive fans back into the casino? No, but the Zamboni became more of a draw than the team. We did get a lot of coverage."

Cooper added that those sweetheart deals for teams like the Thunder would never fly anymore because it would be too hard to prove in today's higher standards

that the ads actually were profitable. Caesars also received two VIP boxes and the 1,200 tickets a game. Cooper gave the seats to Human Resources because "the whales and the guys in the baccarat lounge didn't want them."

The Thunder made many tradeouts to pad the seats. There were reports that there were trade deals with numerous sponsors throughout the city that involved hundreds more tickets, more than 2,000 total per game.

The Thunder games started with the team taking to the ice to the unmistakable sound of AC/DCs "Thunderstruck" blaring throughout the Thomas & Mack Center. The starting lineup introductions included the players skating through pyrotechnics with teal laser shows and ambient fog from the base of a giant slot machine displaying three large Thunder logos. Once the puck dropped, fans were entertained with videos and music like one finds at a rock concert. The loveable and playful polar bear mascot Boom Boom would amp up the energy, leading the passionate fans, choreographing dances, surfing with the Zamboni, and, of course, his T-shirt tosses from the ice between periods.

Midway through the Thunder's fourth season in 1996-97, the Stickney family partnered with former Sony Pictures Chairman Peter Guber and his Mandalay Sports Entertainment on all their baseball and hockey ventures. The partnership made the Stickneys more formidable in baseball, not hockey.

Rumors began to circulate that the Thunder would leave Las Vegas for a new Mandalay-run arena under consideration in Ontario, Calif.

When Ottawa Senators star and former NHL Rookie-of-the-Year Daniel Alfredsson held out in 1997, his agent reached out to the Thunder. But GM Bob Strumm rebuffed Alfredsson's agent with a low offer, later telling The Las Vegas SUN (10/8/1998), "We're not a Club Med for unsigned NHL players. We're not doing that anymore."

But the Thunder did do a repeat. Late in the 1997-98 season, the Thunder signed Pittsburgh Penguins holdout scoring star Petr Nedved. Nedved was one of the elite centers in hockey and Thunder officials hoped he'd lead a Turner Cup playoff run. Nedved was different than Yashin and Joseph because he wasn't just an early season rental. However, the IHL ruled Nedved ineligible to join the team so late in the season, and he appeared in only three regular season games for Las Vegas. Nedved's contract dispute with Pittsburgh dragged into the next autumn. He re-joined the Thunder in the fall of 1998 for 13 games until a trade to the New York Rangers cleared up his contract fight. He was the last world-class player to wear a Thunder jersey.

Poof, They're Gone

The Thunder's lease at Thomas & Mack Arena ended in the spring of 1999. The Thunder closed for business that April, a few days after the conclusion of the team's sixth season. The rest of the IHL folded two years later in May 2001.

Las Vegas sports columnist Ron Kantowski summed up the team's demise in print on April 13, 1999, in the Las Vegas SUN.

The headline read: "Thunder owners made bad choices long ago."

Kantowski wrote: "The most stunning development over the past weekend was not that the Thunder is on its way to folding, leaving town or going dark for next season, but that Thomas & Mack director Pat Christenson somehow is responsible for it.

"That's like saying the guy who rented you a car is to blame when you wrap it around a pole.

"Factions within the Thunder, the IHL and even the local media say Christenson is the bad guy for driving a hard bargain — or no bargain at all— when it came time for the hockey team to negotiate a new lease.

"Whether that's true or not is irrelevant, only because this much is true: The Thunder and UNLV have not seen eye-to-eye on the lease since the franchise's inception.

"So why didn't the Thunder just bite the bullet on its original Zamboni investment and build its own rink five years ago? Or why didn't it talk Mandalay Entertainment into doing the same last year, when the movie moguls came on board as co-owners of the Thunder and Stars?

"Even after Arnold and George Clooney were paid for "Batman The Movie" the Mandalay guys still had to have a few nickels left over for hockey, didn't they?

"That's a question that somebody ... needs to ask," one club official agreed.

"Instead of foolishly spending money on female goalies or disgruntled NHL holdouts looking for a cushy place to while away a contract squabble, the Thunder should have been investing in a home of its own and a full-fledged NHL affiliation.

"That's the formula the Michigan K-Wings have used to become the IHL's second-oldest continuous running franchise.

"The K-Wings play their home games in a closet (K-Wings Stadium seats 5,113), yet the Kalamazoo-based team has managed to survive for 24 years. They get a big assist from the NHL's Dallas Stars, who pay most of the player freight.

"Triple-A baseball works the same way.

"The Las Vegas Stars are considered the only successful pro sports franchise in Las Vegas' checkered history as a pro sports town. But were it not for the Padres' financial support and a sweetheart deal at Cashman Field, they'd be a distant memory, too.

"In retrospect, other than timing the club's formation (either by design or dumb luck) to coincide with a low ebb in the UNLV basketball program when Rollie Massimino replaced Jerry Tarkanian as head coach, the Thunder front office simply didn't have a clue about how to make minor league hockey work here.

"So once the novelty wore off, it only was a matter of time until the Thunder went the way of the Slinky or a Cabbage Patch doll."

Paying Not To Play

By the time they exited the IHL in 1999, the Thunder never won a championship but captured their first two division championships.

Libonati came back to Thomas & Mack during the last year of the franchise. When he viewed the books, he knew the Thunder would not be able to withstand the red ink he saw for himself. They were happy to switch weekend dates to weekdays when Libonati got a better offer from the likes of Bob Arum and Don King.

"I had a lot of hockey game holds on Fridays and Saturdays that were costing me an opportunity to do a big fight, which would make the arena a lot more money than the set fee for the Thunder," he said. "I had hockey games on hold I could postpone, and I could let the Stickney family know that I needed those dates for a boxing match. Sadly, they were OK with working with us. They weren't doing the business, so they welcomed the date changes. We were able to get big events, so they weren't so angry at the changes as you would think."

Switching game dates the last year was a regular occurrence, sometimes with the Thunder calling Libonati and asking him "if they had any other events" to get bumped.

"They loved it because I was paying them 50 grand to move the date," Libonati said. "Fifty grand here, 50 grand there was starting to add up. The bottom line was they couldn't create more revenue on the weekends than I could make with Arum and King. They were taking 50 grand to go away – at least $300,000 total."

Slowly, the fans disintegrated.

"If the product isn't what people expect, don't expect people to come," Libonati said. "People were let down. They were a really good team the first and second year and people had high hopes. They just quit on them. The team wasn't hungry."

'They weren't doing any business at the venue," he said. "After a while, it didn't make sense due to the expenses to keep up the venue. We could make more with a weekend of concerts or fights than we could with 10 to 15 hockey games. When a team drops below a certain level of attendance, it certainly is a recipe for disaster. With a population of just over a half-million people, there weren't enough fans who weren't working to keep up. There are three 8-hour shifts in a 24-hour town. You have one shift to work with."

Libonati saw the franchise slowly melting.

"When the Thunder started out, they were good, they were exciting and they were competitive. If you're not here for the long run, it starts to go badly. They always point the finger at the venue."

The Runnin' Rebels had the same problem after Jerry Tarkanian left.

"Jerry Tarkanian was the only UNLV coach who never pointed the finger at the venue. They pointed the finger at us for failing. That's not a good look. The guy who books the events has a better idea of what will work and won't work."

The Thunder pointed the blame toward T&M for not making changes to accommodate a permanent arena as the reason the relationship ended.

"I laid out the costs for the needed renovation, and it didn't work for us," he said. "The team wasn't half of what it was in the early years. It started out to be fantastic, but then…. I helped get it launched, and I'm also the guy who kills it."

The simple truth: Thunder management failed the franchise.

"Hockey teams, even at the highest levels, think that you owe them something," Libonati said. "Because

Boom Boom, the Thunder's mascot.

I'm bringing you a team, they think you owe them something."

When the venue owns the team or the municipality owns the team, success is more likely.

"It's all well and good when a city or county is bringing you a team," Libonati said. "They all start out happy (like the Thunder). Your marketing is working, there is a nice attendance, and everyone is excited and everyone is happy. As years go by and payrolls grow, and expenses rise, teams point fingers at the bricks and mortar. It's not that their marketing dropped off, or we started losing, or our style of play, the product was bad, or the fans decided not to come. It becomes the bricks and mortar's fault. It's always the venue's fault. But we had to book other shows. We realized we had a chance to put new people in the building with other events."

The management of the Thomas & Mack had seen enough and decided not to make any more renovations. The ending was abrupt. The Thunder was no more.But the early years showed that hockey was going ng going to work somewhere in Las Vegas.going to work somewhere in Las Vegas.

Chapter 7
Miracle on Roller Blades

It was the end of March 1994 and the Aces' season had just come to an end with an impressive 32-11-1 record and a run in the playoffs.

Plans already were in place for the 1994-1995 season, but all would change rather quickly with a visit from two suit-clad gentlemen and three associates who sauntered into the Santa Fe arena one hot afternoon.

Dan Kotler, Cal Coleman, Boris Chiate, Dr. Richard Commentucci and Slava Fetisov descended on Vegas one weekend with one focal point: Plant a new RHI (Roller Hockey International) expansion team in the City of Lights.

On arrival, the only plan was to meet with the IHL Las Vegas Thunder management and convince them that they should wrap their arms around these mega-wealthy hockey buffs, complete with one very proven, professional hockey player, and nearly beg them to be a part of their project.

This may well have happened were it not for the fact that the Stickney family, who owned the Las Vegas Thunder along with a very successful AAA ball team in Vegas, considered themselves to already be poised at the top of the Vegas sports mountain. The Stickney's also were in the middle of building another new AAA club in Rancho Cucamonga that was keeping the family quite busy.

It isn't difficult to figure out the ego levels of all involved when you have the self-proclaimed monarchy of sports families on the West Coast, the Stickneys, doing a meeting with a guy who developed a plastic tile for sports use (Sport Court), Kotler, his buddy and insurance agent in Salt Lake City, Cal Coleman, a Russian entrepreneur investor who sponsors a semi-professional hockey team, Metalurg, Dr. Richard Commentucci of the New Jersey Devils, and Slava Fetisov all at the same table.

Kotler was quite a character and an old-school, self-made success as the founder of Sport Court, an artificial surface initially designed for the sport of basketball to be used either inside or out. The surface was lightweight and easily assembled and disassembled, making it also the perfect surface for any outside special events.

Sport Court was a natural for the sport of inline skating of any type, and with the inception of roller hockey — amateur, collegiate and a fledgling professional

league, the surface became standard for the newly created RHI (Roller Hockey International).

The meeting lasted an entire 15 minutes and ended in a flurry of insults, especially thrown by the two largest egos, Stickney and Kotler. Suffice it to say, the outsiders from New Jersey and Salt Lake City certainly didn't do their homework and left the meeting pretty bruised up.

It was about 1 p.m. at the Sante Fe and after 3-plus hours in a panic over who was going to headman their new franchise, the group descended on the arena where Bob Lawson, arena manager, hockey director and GM of the Las Vegas Aces, was overseeing the installation of a new compressor for the ice-making equipment. The desert heat and zero humidity can wear out equipment designed for an entirely different climate.

The group, all in business suits, hung around for a while until Bob glanced over and recognized a familiar face — Slava Fetisov, one of hockey's greatest of all time and later inductee into the Hockey Hall of Fame.

That one person was enough to get Lawson's attention regardless of who the rest were. As each introduced himself to Lawson, it became apparent they were not there as tourists. They truly had something in mind and something they hoped would put a mark on Las Vegas hockey as well.

They were going with "Plan B," which all smart entrepreneurs, investors and athletes always have. Lawson had no clue what he was about to hear, and surprised he was.

Kotler began with his classic overbearing and arrogant demeanor, laying out what the plan was in planting a new RHI franchise team in Vegas. He explained in broad reference the fact they had tried to field a team (Utah Roller Bees) in the first season but failed horrendously, on the ice and in the wallet. Fact was the Roller Bees were a team basically built around one player, Rich Chernomez, an exceptional talent who not only made the NHL show but played in nearly every league in the U.S. and globally throughout his career. Rich had done his thing for Dan Kotler in Utah, but one man never made an entire team, and Rich was following Kotler to wherever it would take him.

Kotler continued telling Lawson what was going to happen without once explaining how or with whom it was going to be built around.

The funny part was Kotler was trying so hard to impress Lawson; once again, he forgot to do his homework. Lawson is a lifetime career entrepreneur who had just finished a 5-year stint as one of the most successful managers in the world of professional motorcycle racing. He represented riders such as AMA Camel Pro dirt track Champion Jay Springsteen, and AMA & World Superbike Champion Doug Polen. Hockey on roller skates was not too exciting to him at the time.

Feeling the meeting coming to the same conclusion as the prior Stickney meeting, Coleman and Fetisov jumped in. If a guy as noteworthy to hockey as Fetisov was involved, there just might be something tangible, so Lawson continued the meeting.

The meeting became dinner that evening, and that evening led into the next morning as only Vegas can,

and by the end of the night, they had convinced Lawson to get on board as the general manager of an RHI team yet to be named.

The Stickney family's rejection turned out to be a blessing in disguise for the RHI investment group, primarily because of the partnership they formed with Lawson. With Lawson on board, they gained access to a range of valuable assets that positioned their new RHI team for success.

The RHI had league President Dennis Murphy, who had been involved in the establishment of the American Basketball Association, World Hockey Association and World TeamTennis. The RHI hoped to capitalize on the inline skating boom of the early 1990s. Key parts of its attraction to West Coast franchisees were its stance on no-guaranteed contracts and a split of all prize money.

"The RHI was taking the West Coast inline hockey community by storm in the summer of 1993," Lawson recalled. "Dan Kotler and Cal Colman asked to sit down with me with the idea of moving the Utah Roller Bees from Salt Lake City to Las Vegas for the 1994 season. They went on to say they already had transferred the franchise with the RHI. They continued to say they initially figured the Thunder organization would welcome them with open arms, however, they didn't know the Stickneys or GM Bob Strumm that well and made way too many assumptions about how that was going to play out. No need to talk about how those conversations went other than to say the Thunder pretty much snubbed their noses at the whole idea."

The Stickneys passed, but the RHI had one giant asset they overlooked — a TV deal with ESPN. The rules in the RHI were similar to ice hockey. Besides the obvious difference of playing on a floor instead of ice, the RHI had four players and a goalie at a time on the playing surface. Minor penalties were only a minute and a half as opposed to two minutes, and major penalties were four minutes instead of five.

There were no blue lines and, therefore, no offside; however, there was still illegal clearing (icing) and a different version of offside, as a player could skate over the red line before the puck. However, the player couldn't receive a pass over the line. The puck itself was lighter, at 3.5 oz., and was made of red plastic as opposed to a 5.5 oz. black rubber puck. There were four 12-minute quarters as opposed to the NHL's three 20-minute periods. A tied score at the end of regulation time in the regular season would go straight to a shootout instead of overtime.

Lawson was being coerced to run a team in Vegas.

"Kotler went on to say all the things he felt would convince me to take on the project, and quite honestly, it was extremely appealing," Lawson said. "In my mind, hockey had already planted itself in the Vegas hockey community with not one but two professional choices over the 1993-'94 season with the Aces and the Thunder. Putting a Professional Roller Hockey team online with NHL, AHL and IHL players, along with ESPN TV coverage, in an already established three-division league, was a given."

Only one slight hiccup: Kotler made it very clear he wanted to have it all up and running for the first game already scheduled with Phoenix on June 4, 1994, less than 90 days away.

"No problem, I initially thought, since we already had the Roller Bee organization that could easily be moved to Vegas, that was until Kotler and Coleman explained it would be treated like an expansion team, and no one other than the two of them and a couple of players would be joining us," Lawson said.

"We already had a nice hockey fan base in Vegas, but what about everything else? Kotler said, 'No problem.' Just tell Cal what you need, and Cal here will get it for you. Bottom line, Bob, you can do this."

Lawson reached out to those who had just spent the last year developing hockey with the Aces.

He had the following pillars in place:

• Established Player Roster: Lawson brought with him a roster of minor league players who were already familiar with the Las Vegas hockey scene. This foundation of local talent provided the team with a strong starting point.

• Media and Marketing Expertise: Lawson's involvement came with an embedded media and marketing team headed up by Richard Gubbe. This was essential for promoting the team, creating buzz, and engaging with the local community.

• Commercial Sponsorship Base: Lawson's connections with leading business sponsors in the area proved to be an asset. These sponsors provided financial support and resources, contributing to the team's overall success.

• Youth Hockey Program: The presence of a youth hockey program hungry for the sport created a fan base and potential future players for the RHI team. The accessibility of street hockey resonated well with the local community.

• Connections to Professional Hockey: Lawson's extensive network within the world of professional hockey brought credibility and expertise to the team.

With these elements in place, an agreement was etched, and Las Vegas had its newest professional hockey team in the city that never sleeps.

"Richard Gubbe was my number one call, and I will never forget his reaction when we met and I told him about the project. He said, "No problem — we have a full year to put this together." I said, 'Nope....75 days.' That look on his face was priceless, but as a good hockey addict like myself, we agreed that if anyone can do it, we can. As one knows, nothing gets done in Vegas unless you go straight to the top first, so that's exactly what we did. I took the actual team building and logistical side of things, and Gubbe took the marketing and media. The effort was 24/7, literally."

The RHI had many requirements and directives as it related to keeping the entire league in the same direction. The RHI dictated what kind of venue they wanted to have, the type of team roster they would like to see, the leadership team that needed to be organized, and, above all else, the sponsorship activities so there would not be any national or international conflicts with the league. This was as close to the NHL as it comes, including an ESPN deal.

As Gubbe was pulling together nearly every contact he had from his tenure in Vegas, Lawson was busily putting together a team from the ground up.

"Having just put a very successful season behind us with the Aces, I started my team with one thought in mind, 'If it isn't broken, don't change it," Lawson said. "I gathered my Aces good friend Myron Freund to be my assistant GM, and Randy Huartson became director of player personnel."

In addition to the owners Kotler and Coleman, there were three other owners of the Flash that played an important role in the formation of the team – hockey icons Viacheslav Fetisov, Boris Chate and Dr. Richard Commentucci.

Fetisov came from New Jersey Devils fame and also was the captain of the Soviet National Team. Chate was a Russian businessman. Both owned Spartek and Metalurg from the Russian Pro Elite league, which is the Soviet version of our NHL.

Commentucci was the team physician of the New Jersey Devils since their inception and also a hockey addict, having studied with Anatoly Tarasov, the father of Soviet Hockey.

With the season upon them in weeks, Lawson and his management team jumped in with both feet to make the season a reality. The major holes included:
- No place to play.
- No offices to work out of
- No players signed.
- No coaches, trainers, or administrative staff
- No name
- No logo
- No announcer
- No roller hockey surface w/ dasher boards to play on.
- No equipment
- No housing for players
- No sponsorships
- No money

Just four guys, some very fast-talking owners with a lot of promises, and a piece of paper stating we needed to be ready to play within 8 weeks.

Finding A Rink

Only a fool would take on such a challenge, but Lawson and his crew were not only all hockey players; they ate, slept and lived hockey 24/7. From day one, no one was going to tell Lawson or his front office

Outdoor practice at the Thomas & Mac Center.

management team it couldn't be done. With phones a blazing, Lawson was negotiating possible playing locations, and that was only two conversations: Santa Fe, 2,500 seats max, or the Thomas & Mack Center (T&M) at UNLV with 18,000 seats.

Lawson's allegiances to his current Las Vegas Aces ice hockey team and the Santa Fe Arena, his first choice was his current location. However, the RHI was drawing fans from 8,000 to 16,000 per game. That made the Santa Fe too small to use. That narrowed the path to only one facility, the T&M, the home of the Runnin' Rebels.

Not being the shy type, Lawson, with his mentor father, Robert Lawson Jr. (Las Vegas Tournament Sports) in tow, simply drove over to the T&M to introduce himself, where he met Steve Stallworth and Pat Christenson.

They say timing is everything and that statement couldn't have been more accurate than it was the day Lawson, Christenson and Stallworth met and talked about bringing an RHI team to the T&M as home base.

The meeting couldn't have gone any better as it became obvious the relationship the Thunder had with the T&M wasn't quite working out as expected. Christensen ran the venue and Stallworth handled the sales and marketing, and both met with Lawson. Without a lot of detail, Pat and Steve couldn't have been more accommodating, and a deal was cut without hesitation.

"From that point forward, it was nuts," Lawson said. "But in Vegas, the impossible can happen with the right people involved, and we had the right people from the start."

Stallworth has had a distinguished career in Las Vegas, first on the gridiron and then in the sports and entertainment industry. With his outward, down-home country personality, his work experience also included being the vice president and general manager for the Orleans Arena and associate director of the Thomas & Mack Center, Sam Boyd Stadium and Cox Pavilion. With nearly 30 years of event venue experience, Stallworth currently serves as the general manager of the South Point Arena, Equestrian Center and Priefert Pavilion. The South Point Arena is a 4,500-seat multi-purpose arena. The South Point Equestrian Center Complex, which includes two additional arenas as part of the Priefert Pavilion, is widely regarded as the premier equestrian facility in the United States.

When told there had been nearly 30 professional sports franchises in Las Vegas, Stallworth joked, "I was probably involved in 18 of them."

Stallworth also was the director of sports marketing for the UNLV Athletic Department, director of corporate sales for the Canadian Football League's Las Vegas Posse, director of marketing and sales for the Arena Football League's Las Vegas Sting and the Continental Indoor Soccer League's Las Vegas Dust Devils. He also worked with the Las Vegas Thunder, The Las Vegas Wranglers and the Flash.

A 1987 UNLV graduate, Stallworth played quarterback for the UNLV Rebels football team from 1982-'86. He was named team captain and received the scholar athlete award in 1985 and 1986. During his caree, Stallworth threw for 3,789 yards and 23 touchdowns. Stallworth was also named one of the top 100 athletes in the 100-year history of Yuma High School and was elected to the Nevada Sports Hall of Fame in 2019.

Stallworth was the head of sales and marketing back in 1994 when he remembers Lawson coming to the Thomas & Mack looking for a home for the Flash.

"I'm from Yuma, Arizona, and I didn't know what any of this was about," Stallworth recalls of the surge in hockey in Las Vegas in the early 1990s. "This hockey thing, especially roller hockey, was all new to me. It was crazy, but I thought it was fun and exciting. Bob and his guys were ahead of their time."

The only drawback: the arena wasn't available for practice time inside T&M because the Thunder and special events took priority ."Bob said, 'I'll just practice out in the parking lot.'" Stallworth recalled. "That's also where we had car sales out there. I would see these poor kids out there in the middle of summer practicing outside on my way into work."

Hitting the Streets

An office was rented within walking distance from the Thomas & Mack Arena, and the Flash was born. After practice, Lawson pounded the streets for sponsors, but he wasn't alone.

"Bob was such a team guy. He was a hustler," Stallworth said. "He worked with everybody. We loved him to death. I would see Bob all over the city. We were all trying to sell to the same sponsors and sell tickets to the same people. The Sting and the Dust Devils were trying to do the same thing."

Lawson's hard work paid off.

"Sport Court was obviously our primary sponsor and part owner, and provided a complete set of dasher boards, glass and surface to be set up inside the arena, along with another complete setup for practicing the team in the parking lot of the arena,"

Lawson said.

"At that very first meeting, it was decided due to

time issues, we would bring on as many of the Las Vegas Aces management team as possible with longtime Las Vegan Terry Doyle in sales, Frank Salgado trainer, and a few sales and administrative staff," Lawson said. "Utilizing this talent was key to accomplishing this feat."

Kenny Morrow Signs On

With the facility in place, no time could be wasted on formalizing the team roster, including the coaching staff.

"We had to deliver a product that was capable of competing with any type of event, sporting or not, to draw fans and to draw kids," Lawson said, "Something other than just air-conditioning in the desert in the summer."

Lawson knew that he needed a drawing card behind the bench, who not only had the experience but was also a draw himself. That drawing card was Lawson's longtime childhood friend and playing partner, Ken Morrow.

Kenny Morrow and Bob Lawson stand outside the old Showboat Hotel marquee.

THE Ken Morrow was a defenseman with the Gold Medal-winning Miracle on Ice team and four-time Stanley Cup winner with the New York Islanders, with experience taking on a few coaching programs as well. He was and is currenlty employed as one of the Islander's lead Pro Scouts.

"That was a fun call to make, as Kenny and I hadn't spoken in a few years," Lawson recalled. "After all the laughs, especially regarding the time crunch, Ken agreed to take on the challenge, and plans were made to move him to Vegas within the week."

Lawson and Morrow were childhood friends and skating buddies in the same organization growing up and lived less than 6 miles from each other. They were also defensive partners on a Junior All-Star team that played the Toronto Junior Maple Leafs and beat them 2 out of 2 on their home ice, with Morrow scoring a hat trick in both games.

"The call from Bob was a call from my past It was out of the blue," Morrow said in a 2023 interview. "But I thought the offer was really intriguing. I knew there was a roller hockey league going on at that time

and it was really popular. I didn't know much about it other than that."

The timing had to be perfect, as Morrow certainly wasn't going to walk away from the Islanders for the Flash.

"Life as a scout keeps you busy from September through May, which meant my summers were open. In that regard, it fit perfectly," Morrow said. "A lot of the guys we ended up signing were guys I had scouted in the minor leagues, and I knew a lot of the guys who were playing in the roller hockey league. I didn't think it was crazy and I was open to the idea."

Morrow had three years of coaching with stints in the minors in 1989-1990, 1990-1991, and was an assistant with the Islanders in 1991-1992. He was co-coach of the International Hockey League's Kansas City franchise in 1990-1991 and assistant coach of the IHL Flint Spirits in 1989-1990 shortly after retiring from hockey.

"Just the thought of doing something different in the summer and in a great city like Las Vegas for three months — I'm glad he gave me a call," Morrow said. "There were a lot of similarities between the two sports, and the mere fact you were on wheels takes

Ken Morrow hoists one his four Stanley Cups.

Ken Morrow wears his 1980 Olympic Gold Medal.

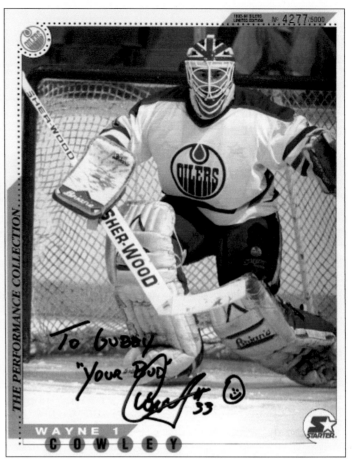

WAYNE 1
COWLEY

some getting used to."

Kenneth Arlington Morrow, born Oct. 17, 1956, is a member of the United States Hockey Hall of Fame. He played 550 regular season games in the NHL between 1980 and 1989.

Morrow was born in Flint and grew up in the nearby town of Davison, Mich. He attended Bowling Green State University where he was a star defenseman and also represented Team USA at the 1978 Ice Hockey World Championships.

His best year as a college player was in 1979 when he was named Central Collegiate Hockey Association Player of the Year.

The following season, Morrow made the 1980 U.S. Olympic hockey team that beat the Soviets before defeating Finland to win the gold medal.

Selected 68th overall in the 1976 NHL Entry Draft by the Islanders, Morrow joined the Islanders immediately after the Olympics. He helped them win their first Stanley Cup in 1980, making him the first player to win the Olympic Gold and an NHL championship in one season. He was an integral member of all four Islanders Stanley Cup teams in 1980, 1981, 1982 and 1983. Although Morrow was never a goal-scorer, during the playoffs, the Isles often benefited from his clutch goal-scoring at key times. Morrow also returned to the United States national team for the 1981 Canada Cup tournament.

His most individual accomplishment in his profes-

sional career was during the 1984 playoff win in Game 7 as his goal beat the New York Rangers. During the 1980 and 1983 playoffs, Morrow had arthroscopic surgeries performed on his knees and played only days afterward in order to contribute to the Islanders championships, often having fluid drained from his knees between games. He was eventually forced to retire prematurely from the game in 1989 due to constant knee problems.

In the 1981 TV movie about the 1980 gold medal-winning U.S. Hockey team called Miracle on Ice, he is played by Scott Feraco. Morrow was portrayed by actor Casey Burnette in the 2004 Walt Disney Studios film "Miracle." Before the movie, Burnette played junior hockey for the Barrie Colts in the Ontario Hockey League, the Hull Olympiques (now called the Gatineau Olympiques) and the Montreal Rocket, both in the Quebec Major Junior Hockey League. Burnette is clean-shaven in the film, although the real Morrow had a beard at the time the film was set.

While most of the players on the team were not allowed to wear facial hair, coach Herb Brooks specifically allowed Morrow to keep his beard since Morrow had a beard prior to joining the team.

Little did anyone realize at the time that Ken's iconic beard would help lead to the "Playoff Beard" pattern of the NHL players years later.

That was the most lenient Brooks ever was and it

paid off selecting Morrow. His blocked shot in front of the net with just over 2 minutes left helped seal the win over the Soviet Union.

With the Flash, Morrow ironically was working for Russian legend Fetisov.

"Putting Kenny together with this ownership team was actually quite exciting in the beginning as we anticipated being able to tap the talent of the Russian teams for their supposedly advanced skating skill," Lawson said.

Kenny Morrow Arrives in Vegas

Morrow was pleased with the T&M even though access was limited.

"Here was a roller hockey team playing in a building like that," Morrow said. There were some drawbacks that popped up. We weren't able to practice in there and we weren't able to use the (Thunder's) boards. It was great except for those 100-degree days and full hockey equipment on the players. We practiced in the parking lot at 6 a.m. and a roller rink (in Henderson) a few times. You had to be flexible and do things on the fly."

When Morrow came to town, building the team quickly took shape. Morrow. Lawson and Huartson started making calls and found out that recruiting players was easier than expected.

"Who wouldn't want to spend the off-season playing the sport they love for Ken Morrow, living in Las Vegas, and getting paid well for a few months before the ice season begins?" Lawson said.

Within a couple of weeks, Morrow, Lawson and Huartson had assembled the initial 18 players needed to start the season, then built upon that as the season went on by adding free agents, trades and a Russian contingent fostered by Fetisov.

"Between the three of us, we had some good connections in hockey," Morrow said. "We were truly an expansion-type setup."

From the USA
- #5 - Myron Freund - D – Player coach, team captain of the Las Vagas Aces, PSHL, and Asst. GM Flash RHI
- #6 - John Grisevich - D – Utah Roller Bees - RHI
- #11 – Paul Snow – F – Utah Roller Bees - RHI
- #44 – Kevin Quinn – D – Johnstown Chiefs – AHL
Leafs – Asst. Coach Flash – RHI

- #10 – Troy Frederick – D – IHL Kansas City Blades
- #19 – Ross Harris – F – AJHL
- #22 – Todd Harris – D – ECHL Birmingham
- #33 – Wayne Cowley – G – NHL (Edmonton Oilers, Calgary Flames), IHL Salt Lake City, AHL

Miss Flash models a home jersey in a promo ad.

Cape Briton, Canadian Olympic Team
- #35 – Scott Brower – G – Elite League of Finland
- #37 – Serge Roberge – F – NHL Quebec Nordiques
- #94 – Scott Daniels – F – NHL Hartford Whalers, AHL Springfield Indians

From Canada
- #16 - Rich Chernomaz – F – NHL (New Jersey Devils, Calgary Flames, Colorado Rockies) – IHL Salt Lake Golden Eagles – AHL St. Johns Maple Leafs – Asst. Coach Flash – RHI
- #10 – Troy Frederick – D – IHL KC
- #19 – Ross Harris – F – AJHL
- #22 – Todd Harris – D – ECHL Birmingham
- #33 – Wayne Cowley – G – NHL (Blades, Oilers, Calgary Flames), IHL Salt Lake City, AHL Cape Briton, Canadian Olympic Team
- #35 – Scott Brower – G – Elite League of Finland
- #37 – Serge Roberge – F – NHL Quebec Nordiques
- #94 – Scott Daniels – F – NHL Hartford Whalers, AHL Springfield Indians

From Russia
- #15 – Sergey Devyatkov – F – REL (Russian Elite League) Metalurg
- #77 – Dmitriy Filippov – F – REL Metalurg
- #28 – Evegnviy Gubarev – D – REL Metalurg
- #7 – Yuriy Isayev – D – REL Metalurg
- #66 – Konstantin Isakov – D – REL Metalurg
- #55 – Alexei – Pogodin – F – REL Metalurg

After a few weeks and through the season, the following would join the Flash Roster.

- Walt Poddubny – NHL – Edmonton Oilers, New Jersey Devils, Toronto Maple Leafs
- Brent Fleetwood – WHL, ECHL, AHL
- Stu Kulak – NHL Vancouver, Edmonton, Quebec
- Shawn Heaphy – IHL Las Vegas Thunder
- Rob Pallin – PSHL Las Vegas Aces
- Steve Chelios –ECHL – AHL
- Garth Snow – NHL Quebec
- Bill Grum – IHL Toledo
- Eric Danielson – PSHL Las Vegas Aces
- Steve Herniman – IHL Kalamazoo, Ft. Wayne
- Gary Daniels – WHL
- Dan Greene – PSHL Las Vegas Aces

"We thought we ended up having the best team on paper with a handful of guys who played high-level NHL and minor league hockey. There were good players from AHL, IHL and ECHL, and a few from the NHL," Morrow said. "On paper, we had a really good team, but it didn't necessarily translate to roller hockey well. The teams that did better in the league were packed with lower minor league guys. They were a bit hungrier. They had to fight and claw their way into making money any way they could. We had a lot of talented ice hockey guys, but the lower minor leaguers were more eager to make some extra money."

Rich Chernomaz was a star in the AHL. Wayne Cowley, Walt Poddubny, Steve Kulak, Garth Snow and Scott Daniels had vast NHL experience. Steve Chelios was the younger brother of Hall of Famer Chris Chelios.

"The RHI was not a flash in the pan," Morrow said. "Kind of like arena football. "It almost grew too fast. It exploded. Lightning in a bottle for the league. We were playing in Anaheim and they sold out the building at 16,000. There were pockets of California where it was very popular."

"With Morrow now on board, he and Huartson worked diligently in putting a team together, and the final list read pretty strong, but time was against us as getting over 25 players to Las Vegas, into apartments, and practice now became the challenge," Lawson said.

"At this point and seeing everything taking place, two amazing individuals and true Las Vegans came through and started making introductions for me," Lawson said. "Pat Christenson and Steve Stallworth reached out to nearly every commercial sponsor they knew. Had it not been for these two assisting at this level, one could truly say the Flash would have been dead in their tracks."

By the end of Week 5, Lawson had over $1M committed from sponsorships, and once the big ones came on board, others joined in. By the time of the first game, the Flash was one of the most commercially sponsored teams of all the new franchises in the RHI.

With Gubbe's promotions under way, and the media blitz out, the city started to pick up on the hype. Huartson performed miracles with CCM getting the jerseys in record time, while putting together minor equipment sponsors to provide us with enough equipment to at least field the initial team.

"Just 10 days past signing the agreement with the owners, we announced the Flash," Lawson said. "The name and the logo were representative of a Desert Dragon on inline skates, derived from Nevada Native American Folklore. The logo was accepted by the owners, and boy, did we run with it."

Forming Partnerships

While the player rostering was taking place, the Flash marketing, media and promotions team was definitely burning the midnight oil, literally.

"The toughest part of my job was convincing the local media that these were actual hockey players, many of whom had NHL credentials," Gubbe said. "The writer with the most savvy was Bill Liesse, sports editor of the Las Vegas SUN. Bill wrote the most about the Flash in print media and followed every game. He understood the skill level and the entertainment value. We lost him to an aortic rupture on Jan. 2, 2016. He was a true professional."

"From day one, the local media was awesome when it came to the Flash with nearly daily announcements and promotion coverage of what you would expect to see at the NHL level," Lawson said. "Of course, it was an easy pitch when you have a lineup of current NHL greats either playing, coaching, or running these off-season RHI teams."

Players such as Bryan Trottier, Al Secord, Rik Wilson, Corrado Micalef, Matt DelGuidice, Walt Poddubny, Craig Coxe and Daniel Berthiaume. Along with future NHLers who played in the RHI, including Darren Langdon, Manny Legace, Steve Poapst, Mike Kennedy, Harry York and Glen Metropolit. Not to mention the NHL coaches such as Bernie Federko, Roy Sommer, Al MacIsaac, Yvan Cournoyer, Chris McSorely, Robbie Nichols, and Las Vegas Flash Gold Medal, 4-time Stanley Cup Champion Ken Morrow.

Within three weeks left to go before the initial puck drop at the Thomas & Mack, the Flash had 34 corporate sponsorships, both local and national, along with 24 of Las Vegas and Nevada media sponsors. The list included Coca-Cola, Snapple, Nevada Beverage, Prestige Travel, CCM, Cooper and the Showboat Hotel-Casino, along with more than 20 media sponsors.

With all that in place, the team was doing promotions everywhere in the Valley from radio and TV spots to onsite promos giving away merchandise, photographs, autographs, and special seating tickets. It was at one of these live radio events that Lawson met radio personality Ron Garrett, also the Director of Marketing of Circus Circus Casino Resort.

Lawson and Garrett hit it off immediately, which also led to Garrett jumping in and becoming the primary commercial sponsor of the Flash with Circus Circus. This sponsorship became the cornerstone of the success in the Vegas Community, and more so with Circus World of Sports, a regional TV interview sports show hosted by Garrett, who had Lawson on several times promoting the Flash. This relationship grew as the season began, and Circus Circus, through Garrett, launched several promotions for the Flash with appearances in the theme park and special events.

"Securing primary sponsorship from well-recognized entities like Circus Circus, and Nevada Beverage, along with the support of the Thomas & Mack Arena as the team's home venue, played a crucial role in establishing the Las Vegas Flash as a credible and competitive presence in the sports landscape. In the world of professional sports, credibility is a valuable asset that can influence fan engagement, media coverage, and the overall success of a team.

"The partnership with recognized sponsors and a prestigious venue helped the Las Vegas Flash gain a competitive edge in Roller Hockey International and establish itself as a significant player in the local sports scene," Lawson said. "In May 1994, you would be hard pressed to go anywhere on any day or weekend and not see the Flash logo or players building the hype to the first game."

Roller Hockey Anyone?

The final plastic tile was placed in the floor as fans were starting to tailgate in the parking lot of the arena.

"Tailgate?" at a hockey game, hell yes, one of the major pluses of playing in the off season summer months." Lawson said.

Garrett helped pack the seats with some of Nevada's most notable people. These VIPs ranged from top casino executives to the gold star entertainers who live and perform on a regular basis in Vegas.

The T&M had one of the largest-attended RHI games that evening in the history of the league and the opening show was set to match the hype.

The doors open at the Thomas & Mack with fans filtering in for what will be the record game in the RHI that night with just over 10,000 sold tickets for the opener.

The teams are ready, the pyro display locked and loaded, the concessions abuzz with the Flash merchandise, and the opening performers are all set to go.

With a full fireworks display that would make small towns jealous, and Miss Flash, Las Vegas Cheerleaders, and the Infamous Puck Drop from the T&M ceiling by Bungee Cord, the show was in full swing. However, sometimes even the best plans can be stricken by Murphey's Law, and that's exactly what happened.

It goes without saying you can't just have a standard hockey game opener with an organ player and an anthem singer. Neil Diamond Impersonator "Jay White" was brought in to light up the crowd to sing "Coming to America" and the National Anthem.

With the music ramping up and the cheerleaders running up and down the steps throwing out shirts and souvenirs, the players were making their way down the tunnels to the rink. On the other side, the referees were staged to take the rink first as soon as the pyro goes off.

"The music heightens and White belts out "Coming to America" like it's never been done in any arena anywhere," Lawson said.

"While the fans are all standing and singing along toward the crescendo, the pyro starts slowly and it builds along with the music, the special lighting effects are all in play thanks to Pat Christenson, and Steve Stallworth from the Thomas & Mack."

"White's tribute to Diamond was and is sanctioned by the legendary singer.

"Jay White was incredible, and the indoor Pyro was just as amazing – at least the fans thought so," Lawson said. "Who would have thought the pyrotechnics would cause a slight humidity issue that would put a little moisture on the Sport Court surface. If you know anything at all about inline skating, you know the wheels are not made for moisture, and especially any moisture alone that is lying on a plastic surface."

"With all the hype, the music, the pyrotechnics, no one even considered the fact that when the officials went flying in different directions including airborne, it wasn't just another special effect of the show," Lawson recalled. "Guess we should have checked out the floor while sitting in a heated arena with air-conditioning running all day and the by-product of pyrotechnics also creating a foggy mist in the cold air. Not only were the officials flailing their arms and legs in every direction, but anyone higher than the first 10 rows couldn't see them anyway. Since no injuries happened and the officials frankly laughed as well, it was one hell of referee entrance."

With the referees about to take the surface with a downhill ramp from the locker room area to gain speed before coming out in front of the full house for the start of the game, the fans thought it was part of the opening show when the three officials hit the surface and went airborne with feet and arms swinging every which way imaginable."

"Thank goodness they had protection gear on and no one was injured, but boy oh boy, was that a sight,"

Lawson said. "Had technology been in 1994 what it is today, that video would have gone viral by the end of the game. The officials played it off like the professionals they were, and one of them even went on a put on a little show like he was falling again after the first half of the game.

That was only the beginning of an unexpected and near-tragic fanfare.

"We should have taken it as a sign because the next part of the opening show was to have the puck dropped from the ceiling of the Thomas & Mack by our local Bungee sponsor," Lawson recalled. "I wonder why no one thought about what would happen to a giant rubber band left in the ceiling rafters of an arena with a metal roof at 100-plus degrees outside."

With the huge blowers working to remove the fog and the industrial fans on the floor with teams of workers with mops and paper towels, after 30 long minutes, it was now time to reload what was left in the show and carry on.

With White singing an amazing rendition of the Anthem, the players set up their lines and skated toward the center circle for the puck drop. This was going to be a first ever, as one of the local sponsors was a Bungee Jump Company on the Strip. The idea was to drop the first puck from a bungee drop from the ceiling of the Thomas & Mack.

With 100 degrees against a metal roofed building with a bungee cord in the rafters after testing in the morning against more mild temperatures is not a good formula for a highly calculated jump distance to the center circle.

Anthem ended, centers from each team, along with the head referee at the center circle, and with the drum cadence beating, all eyes went to the ceiling for the puck drop jump.

"On opening night, a couple of bungee jumpers dropped from the rafters of the Thomas & Mack Center to deliver the game puck," Gubbe recalled. "The bungee cords expanded due to the heat, and all I remember was hearing one of the bungee jumpers landing on his tailbone. He had to be helped off the rink. Then came a second jumper."

The Bungee employee took her position with the puck in hand, and with everyone starting to chant the countdown from the time clock, the jump happened. From the time she stepped forward, everything went into slow motion, and the thought of the rubber bungee being in the sweltering heat of the ceiling for the last 10 hours didn't pass anyone's thought process. At least not until she bounced off the floor on her chest and then recoiled up and did it again, and again until someone grabbed her.

"Once again, the fans jumped to their feet, not from what they just witnessed, but because they all thought it was planned," Lawson said. "The beautiful and admirable part was the young laady, who could have benn hurt badly, jumped up and raised her arms like she just won some championship herself. What a trooper!!!

The rest of the game went on without a hitch. This was an opening night many of us will never forget."

By the grace of God, there were no major injuries when the young lady stood high in the ceiling and, to the drum roll, launched herself toward the center rink to deliver the puck.

"When you mention the opening game of the Flash at the T&M Arena, no one can tell you about the game, but they will share either how great Jay was as Neil Diamond, the referees flailing around in the air and spinning into the dasher boards, or of course the delivery of the puck via bungee," Lawson said.

Morrow was in awe.

"There was some definite Las Vegas showmanship," he said. "I was nervous every time he came down.

The crowd got revved up when the team lineups were introduced over Queen's "Flash."

"It was quite an electric opening," Gubbe said. "The fans were into it. The pre-game hype helped to make all the home games exciting."

Although the opener was a hard act to follow, each home game was hyped to the max, and the crowd always responded, win or lose.

How Many Russians Did You Ask For?

Before the start of the season, owner Boris Chate had convinced the other owners his top players on the Metalurg team would fit in perfectly with the Flash players. In addition, since Kenny Morrow and Fetisov had a relationship, Morrow agreed with Huartson to bring them on board.

"My only issue was that we had an apartment sponsor, and I knew they were at the limit with what we already had and how the guys we already had there were breaking the rules," Lawson said. "Not a surprisc from hockey players, especially NHL hockey players."

The complex was trying to be accommodating, and they were one of the nicest apartments in the Green Valley area just off Warm Springs and Eastern.

"As soon as Kenny agreed, Boris was on the phone setting it up for the four players to join us," Lawson

said. "We did speak with the apartment sponsor, and he said he would give us one more two-bedroom for the four players, but 'they better damn well follow the rules or the whole team will be on the street.'"

Usually, when players come in from out of the country, they come with clothing, and some equipment such as their own skates and preferred sticks.

"About 10 days go by, and we are into our third week of gameplay, and Kenny says we need to send the van to the airport to get the Russians."

Huartson grabs the equipment manager, Gary Sbraccia, and Frank Salgado, the trainer, and takes the van to the airport. About a half hour passes and a phone call comes in with an aggravated Huartson. He confirms that eight Russians got off the plane with no clothing, no hockey gear, and no money.

"Not to mention they haven't eaten in three days," Lawson said. "An immediate call goes into Boris with no answer. So Slava gets the call…..still no answer, so Cal Coleman is next. Cal is speechless and simply says take them all to the two-bedroom apartment and he will cover whatever is needed. Eight players, hungry as hell, smelling like hockey players who haven't washed for days."

Soon after, all hell breaks loose.

"It's a Thursday, and we have a game the next night," Lawson said. "I don't remember what call actually came first since they were so close together. One came from Boris Chate, and one from the landlord kicking the entire team out on the street. I did talk the landlord into letting the original team stay, but he was emphatic about the Russians all being out, including the original six who were already there. By the time Kenny Morrow and I finally got to the apartment complex, everything the original rRussians had was on the street physically, along with the other eight who just got there!"

Calls were put out to the youth howdy ockey programs looking for families who might temporarily let a few players board with them.

"To my surprise, they did find families for most of them, and for the others, we negotiated a separate apartment complex to come on board as a sponsor," Lawson said. "After sending home half of the Russian players for a variety of reasons, all seemed to be settling down, but I should have known better."

Only one of the 15 Russians who came over during the season spoke English, and that was very broken English. It's always a great idea to befriend the local authorities if responsible for any kind of sporting group or team.

Especially when law enforcement gets involved.

"Many people in the Vegas Valley didn't know that John Moran, the local Sheriff of Clark County, was a fan of hockey, but he was," Lawson recalled. "I remember the call at 2 a.m. from the Clark County Sheriff's office asking me to come down for a situation regarding the Russian players. I did what a good GM would do; I called my player personnel director, Randy Huartson, and told him to take care of it."

No one expected the forthcoming charge.

"What a surprise the next day when I was told the players had been arrested for shoplifting lady's lingerie to send back to their Russian sweethearts or to sell in the black market," Lawson said. "Randy went on to say that we owed the sheriff some tickets. You bet they were delivered the next day."

That was the way the season went. As the games piled up, the Flash won some, lost some, but the games were always entertaining and high scoring, both home and road. Then came the trip to Vancouver.

The Black Magic of the VooDoo

Although the Flash was short-lived, other franchises in the RHI had a good run and became fan favorites. One such place was Vancouver, with a team aptly named the VooDoo, owned by the NHL's all-time leader in penalty minutes, Tiger Williams.

The home games for the VooDoo were patterned after the Quincy Blue Devils of Illinois High School basketball fame that led to the raucous opening of teams like the Chicago Bulls. The Blue Devils were a highly successful basketball-dominant school along the Illinois-Missouri border in the southwestern part of the state. No school wanted to play there because Quincy would wait until nearly tip-off time and then turn out the lights and blacken the arena with wild music to whip the crowd into a frenzy. Then came the swirling light show. The opposing team would become intimidated, and the Blue Devils would go on to kick some ass and have you beaten before the first quarter ended.

The Bulls took that theme and ran with it, but none made it more intimidating than the Vancouver VooDoo. The franchise had the famous enforcer and bad boy Williams as one of its owners. Tiger's job in the NHL was to fight, and leading the league in penalty minutes was his calling card.

The Flash were known for fighting and skating, and the VooDoo were known for beating people up. The VooDoo had three players the ilk of Williams in Rob Dumas (75 penalty minutes, Lauire Billiek (72 penalty minutes), Brett Thurston (59 penalty minutes), and others who weren't afraid to mix it up. The Flash had tough guys in the Daniels brothers, Serge Roberge,

Myron Freund and Kevin Quinn (85 ninutes), all of whom never backed down from a melee. The Flash also had winger Rich Chernomaz (63 penalty minutes) and Steve Chelios, the younger brother of Chris Chelios, an NHL Hall of Famer.

The younger Chelios was a marginal roller hockey player and bad boy on and off the ice. He was later traded to the Chicago Wolves for a set of roller blades that the league put a news blackout on the deal.

"We traded a player for a set of chassis that go on your skates," Morrow recalled.

"We traded him because he couldn't stop well on roller blades," Lawson said. "Randy Huartson made the deal but we couldn't publicize it."

Flash Coach Ken Morrow was a gentleman coach not known for being fiery or intimidating. He didn't allow swearing in public and reprimanded any player who said the word "shit" loud enough for anyone to hear. The team had a dress code on trips and everyone had a calm demeanor.

"In the early NHL days, you wore a suit and tie," Morrow said. "That may have changed a lot now at all levels. The players all understood it wasn't going to be guys in shaggy-looking sweatsuits or jeans. The RHI was a professional league, and that was the way I approached everything. We had good leaders on the team with Rich Chernomaz and Wayne Cowley. Good character guys, good hockey players."

As Lawrence Taylor used to say, Vancouver had a pack of crazed dogs. Those crazed dogs went 11-2-1 that year. The team played in the PNE Agrodome in 1993 and 1994, and the Pacific Coliseum in 1995. In 1996, the team played in General Motors Place after being sold to Orca Bay Sports and Entertainment, but folded in 1996. Sellouts throughout their tenure were the norm. The VooDoo experienced consistent success in the regular season throughout their four-year history, winning their division all four years. Despite their regular season success, however, the VooDoo never made it out of the second round of the playoffs. The arena was filled for the Flash game. The lights went out, and the crowd was whipped into a frenzy. After the puck was dropped, the Flash wanted to skate. The VooDoo wanted to rumble. Fights broke out, and then Thurston leveled a Flash player with a two-handed crosscheck to the back of his head, and all hell broke loose. Benches cleared, and the fight looked more like the rumble in West Side Story than a hockey fight. The officials lost control completely.

"Our Russian guys were taking shots with guys running at them," Morrow said, recalling the event nearly 40 years later. The referees, I felt, were letting them get away with it."

Lawson added, "Tiger hated the Russians."

"I was standing next to Kenny Morrow when the fight broke out," team PR Director Richard Gubbe recalled. "The normally composed coach who was famous for winning and not fighting became incensed. He called over an official, grabbed him by the collar at the throat, twisted it, and pulled the ref into him. He yelled at him, 'Get the fuck out there and do something.'"

The referee was stunned.

"Not one of my better moments," Morrow admitted. "They were taking some runs at our guys and we had some really tough guys on our team. It was typical of Tiger Williams teams, and I was annoyed that they wanted to play that way. I was over near the door and grabbed some ref and got kicked out."

"Morrow then pushed the referee backward," Gubbe said. "Then Kenny got tossed from the game and tossed from the arena. I had to physically escort him out and into the back of the arena."

"It went way over the top. When their livelihood is playing ice hockey, you don't want these guys getting hurt playing a roller hockey game. It was out of character for me because I was known for being levelheaded," Morrow said. "It was very frustrating and I was young. But the refs lost control, and so did I."

Fans in Vancouver witnessed the only time Morrow ever got tossed from any game, player or coach.

"Never before or since," he said.

As the brawl went on, Gubbe stayed with the coach.

"I sure didn't want to see him go back out there," he said. "He was both angry and disconsolate. At first, I had to physically restrain him. After he cooled off, he realized he had lost it and was saddened by what he did. I can't say as I blamed him. The violence was more than I ever saw in a game and 10 times worse than 'Slapshot.'

Gubbe's brother, Peter, came on the trip to take in his first RHI contest.

"I was stunned," he said. "To see Coach Morrow grab the ref was surreal. The brawls went on for a long time. It was like a gang fight."

Not only did the Flash lose the fight, they lost the game.

As if the Russian players didn't suffer enough, they were held up at the airport when it came time to re-enter the U.S.

"The players didn't have the paperwork as we were going to leave and don't have the proper visas," Lawson recalled. "We were talking about the staff staying behind and going to the embassy."

Then Lawson called Paul Lowden, whom he knew from his days at the Santa Fe. Lowden had the political clout nationally to get them released. On the flight back to Vegas, the team and the coach acted as if nothing had even happened.

Just another game in the RHI.

Where's the Money???

The art of negotiation was never done any better than with Lawson's team of professionals. All of the targeted bullet points had been hit except the support of the ownership.

"Dan Kotler, Boris Chiate, Slava Fetisov, and Richard Commentucci all had the resources to fund this team out of their pockets easily, but the four of them treated this as another toy they expected everyone else to do it for them," Lawson said.

However, there was one additional partner who stepped up to his responsibilities, and that was Cal Coleman.

"I'm sure when he was first involved, Cal didn't anticipate that he would be the sole 'Check Writer' of the Fab Five owners, but it certainly turned out that way," Lawson said.

Of the initial $25K, Lawson chose to pay his people first and take nothing. Without much detail, this never changed, right on through the end when Kotler and the group walked away owing Lawson tens of thousands of dollars.

"I was at all the Flash games," Stallworth said. "There were big crowds for all their games."

Problem was, commercial sponsorship, although necessary for housing, transportation, equipment and merchandising, isn't cash in the bank. Teams such as the Flash can do everything right and unless the owners support the team, it can end as fast as it started.

"I thank Bob Lawson for bringing me out," Morrow said. "It was an amazing time getting to know the city mid-'90s and having my family come out. A summer I will never forget. We can all look back at it and laugh. It was quite the adventure and I'm glad I got to do it."

The RHI had grown to 24 teams in its second year, the only year for the Vegas franchise. Then the league shut down in 1998 and reopened in 1999 with eight teams.

After 1999, the league was no more. The collapse of the RHI stemmed from the NHLPA creating a rule that would not allow NHL players to participate in the RHI without losing their NHLPA insurance.

The story that began only a few months prior sounded like a team planning to play for years in the "City of Lights." Sad to waste a strong fan base that was built by the support for a team such as the Flash.

Chapter 8
Prison Night and Pajamas

The Las Vegas Wranglers created a long-running, successful franchise through traditional and out-of-the-box promotions and a new, dedicated hockey venue. After the Las Vegas Thunder had no place to play anymore, there was a void to fill, and the Wranglers jumped on the horse and made it happen by riding into The Orleans and taking promotion to a level never seen before in pro hockey, or any pro sports franchise for that matter.

The winding road to get to the first puck drop was rocky and filled with rattlesnakes, however.

The story begins with casino mogul Michael Gaughan and his determination to get an arena built and a team to play in it at The Orleans Hotel and Casino. The journey started with Gaughan reaching out to the man who knew all about building a sports franchise – Steve Stallworth, who had the most experience of anyone in Las Vegas.

"In 2001, Michael Gaughan calls me and said he wants to build an arena at The Orleans," Stallworth recalled in 2023. "I said, 'Sir, we need another arena in this town like a hole in the head.' He said I want to do this differently; I want to own a minor league hockey team. We are going to sell beer for $2, hot dogs for $1 and free parking. He wanted it to be for the locals. The more he talked, the more I was in. He sucked me right in. He knew that was what I was all about."

Building an arena was the easy part of the equation.

"My job was to go out and buy a team," Stallworth said. "He knew I knew how to run these teams. I went right to the West Coast Hockey League and the guy who had the rights to a team."

His name was Charles Davenport. He was based out of San Diego and he owned the Bakersfield team with a partner and he also owned the Fresno WCHL team outright.

"I told him I'd like to buy a team. He said I can't buy a team because he had the rights to Vegas. He said he already signed a deal to go with Boyd Gaming to build an arena downtown. I said, 'I want you to know we are going to buy a team.'"

A setback, but only the beginning of a prolonged gun battle.

"I then had to go to the Central Hockey League," Stallworth said. "I had to travel all around the country. We were at the all-star game in Corpus Christi, Texas, and we came to terms with the purchase of a team. Our head coach was going to be Clint Malarchuk. He was a goalie and a cowboy. We hadn't offered it to him, but we had conversations with him. We had everything dialed in there."

Stallworth was running out of options.

"All of a sudden, I get a call from Jim Lites. Lites, who was the president and CEO of the Arizona Coyotes, had heard about what we were doing and said, "Why don't we bring an AHL team there?' I said, Jimmy, that would be amazing."

The Central League was single A, The West Coast was AA, and the AHL was AAA, the last step before the NHL.

"We got it all worked out with what we were going to do," Stallworth said. "We had a deal in principle. Me and Michael Gaughan flew down to Phoenix. Steve Ellman was the owner (of the Coyotes) at the time and ended up bankrupting the whole organization. He started their downfall. We were in a big conference room, and they just kept asking for more stuff, and Michael Gaughan kept saying yes and yes. I kept looking at Michael and saying we are going to lose our ass at this stage. But he was the owner. Michael was going to build a 5,000-square-foot training facility and office. He was going to give every single Coyotes season ticket holder a weekend stay at The Orleans. God bless him; he was amazing. He just kept going on and on."

The Coyotes then pulled the rug out from under them.

"We took a little break, and then Steve Ellman came back in and said, 'Michael, we are further apart than we have ever been.' I had my sport coat on the chair, and Michael looked at me and said, 'Steve, grab your coat, we're out of here.' Jimmy Lites (part of the negotiating team) chased us all the way to the car. He said we could go back to the original deal, and he called me for a week. I said, 'Jimmy, here's the problem, Michael isn't doing this for the money. He wants to go to the arena and enjoy himself. He wants to take his kids and his grandkids. He wants to be proud when he walks in there. I said he'll never have that feeling with you guys.'"

That was the end of a possible AAA affiliation.

"Now we're back to square one," Stallworth said. "We have the CHL back here. So, we had to shit or get off the pot."

With the Las Vegas Thunder of the International Hockey League folding following the 1998-1999 IHL season, the West Coast Hockey League (WCHL) announced its intentions to keep ice hockey in the Las Vegas Valley when they granted expansion rights to the city in 1999, with plans for the team to start competing in the 2000-2001 WCHL season.

The Wranglers team name and logo were announced shortly before what was supposed to be the franchise's inaugural season in 2000, but the team had to suspend its entrance into the WCHL for three seasons due to the lack of a suitable arena.

Deciding not to miss out on another season, the Wranglers announced in October 2002 that they planned to play at the proposed Las Vegas Events Center in Downtown Las Vegas and share the arena with the Community College of Southern Nevada's men's and women's basketball teams. The Events Center was to be paid for and operated by a non-profit organization that was supported by Las Vegas Mayor Oscar Goodman.

Soon after, Ron Kantowski wrote an article on May 23, 2002. The sportswriter, then working for the Las Vegas SUN, wrote a column that cites the downtown arena plans are "On Ice," and Davenport should look to The Orleans as a place to play. In his column, Kantowski wrote:

"Unless a money man steps forward soon, or alternate financing can be arranged, it would seem the

Steve Stallworth

downtown arena has about as much chance of being built as somebody from the Charlestown Chiefs being awarded the Lady Byng Trophy for sportsmanship."

"Honestly, we remain loyal to downtown," Davenport said. "They want a hockey team, and we want to make sure that happens. I'm as confident as I ever was."

"Perhaps Davenport should be penalized two minutes for wishful thinking.

"But he said as long as ground on the downtown arena is broken by late summer or early fall, there should be enough time to complete the building by fall/winter 2003, when Davenport's WCHL Las Vegas expansion franchise — to be known as the "Wranglers" — drops the puck.

"When asked if he had a Plan B in the event that the only ground that winds up being moved downtown is by the wind, he said there was no need to consider one yet.

"But if/when that time comes ("when" is about a minus-360 favorite), the new 7,000-seat arena Michael Gaughan is putting up in The Orleans' parking

lot would be a good one. In fact, it should have been Davenport's Plan A from the start.

"Davenport said he had cursory discussions with Orleans officials about their hockey plans but eventually committed to downtown because — how's this for irony? — he wasn't totally sure The Orleans would go forward with its arena.

"Steve Stallworth, the former UNLV quarterback who is barking signals for The Orleans Arena as its director, said The Orleans is still passionate about minor league hockey, maybe just not as passionate about owning a club itself, which was the original strategy.

"Still, at this point, yes, we will have a hockey team," Stallworth said. "We don't have anything booked, per se, but a lot of things are on hold."

"So not much has changed. It's apparent from the photos on its website that The Orleans will have an arena, but for now, there's no team. And while downtown has a team, for now — and maybe forever — there's no building.

"But it's still not too late to get the peanut butter together with the jelly.

"Maybe that's something we should be looking into," Davenport said."

Whether Davenport had an epiphany, took Kantowski's advice or just came to his senses, Stallworth gets a call from the AA franchise.

Davenport says to Stallworth in a phone call, "Maybe this is something we should be looking into."

"I said to him, 'We don't have a team yet, but we have a lot of things that are on hold.'" Stallworth said. "Charles had committed to downtown, but downtown was just not going to happen."

Stallworth was persistent.

"I kept telling Charles that we had shovels in the ground and steel in the air," he said. "That's when I called Charles and said, 'isn't it time to get the peanut butter with the jelly.' And he said yes. That's when we brought Charles to the table. He already had a team name and a logo. He had everything – a beautiful setup."

The venture was anything but smooth sailing.

"He set me up with his general manager in Fresno to help build the locker rooms and offices — all inside the building. We had this rocking and rolling. About a month before the season starts, Charles calls me and says, 'Listen, I'm bringing a new general manager in, and can you help him get acclimated to the city?'"

In walks Billy Johnson.

"This guy walks in my office in 2003, and he doesn't shake my hand. He doesn't say, 'Hi, how are you?' He drops a piece of paper on my desk and says, 'These are 10 reasons this team will fail in your arena.'"

Johnson had experience with a city-run team, not with a private casino owner.

"From that day forward, it never was a good relationship," Stallworth said. "I was not a fan. Billy was coming from minor league baseball in a city where the city council and councilmen were all subsidizing the venue. This was a new thing for him. This was a private owner, a private casino and a private hotel. There was no city council. I said, 'Billy, I'm your city council. It's not going to be the same as your minor league baseball team.' Billy was very creative, and he brought in a lot of bodies, but it was a tough relationship after that. But that was the way we got the hockey team there."

One more flaw. The Orleans only had one locker room per team.

"When Coach Glen Gulutzan came in, he asked, 'who designed the locker rooms?' I said, 'It was the guy from Fresno.' He said that was all wrong. These guys need two locker rooms – one to put all their street clothes and one for their dirty, smelly-ass player clothes because there is no worse smell in the world than a smelly hockey room."

The situation was not ideal for Stallworth, but he chose the draw of an AA team over owning a Central League franchise.

"In hindsight, we should have owned a team that we could have controlled the team, the product and the experience. But we thought it was better to have a West Coast Hockey League team than own a Central League team."

Stallworth knew the AA team would be a better draw.

"One thing I know, and Gubbe, you know, these hockey fans are loyal as could be," he said. "It didn't matter if it was a Sunday night or a Tuesday night; there were going to be at least 2,5000 fans in the stands every game. It doesn't surprise me at all that the Golden Knights have been that successful. I learned that early on, even with the Thunder, they were loyal fans."

The franchise announced in September 2002 that it was moving to The Orleans Arena that was under construction at The Orleans Hotel and Casino. The Orleans Arena became the home of the Wranglers beginning with the 2003-04 WCHL season. Later, in September 2002, a planned merger between the WCHL and the East Coast Hockey League was announced that would have the WCHL's six active franchises and three expansion franchises (including the Wranglers) join the ECHL for the 2003-2004 season.

From 2003 to 2014, the Wranglers played their home games on the west side of the city at The Orleans Arena. The team's lease with Orleans Arena ended after the 2013-2014 season.

The Wranglers had been the ECHL affiliate of the NHL's Calgary Flames since the team's inaugural season in 2003 until 2009 before announcing that they were switching their affiliation to the Phoenix Coyotes for the 2009-2010 ECHL season.

Let The Promos Begin

Taking advantage of the Las Vegas landscape, the Wranglers were the only pro team to hold a game that was played at midnight. The annual "Midnight Round-up" was created by Johnson so Las Vegas residents who work during the usual game times (employees of the gaming industry), could watch a game. Fans wore pajamas to the game.

"I went to one of their midnight games against Bakersfield," recalled longtime Las Vegas sportscaster Tony Cordasco. "They said the games were to accommodate swing shift workers, but it was mostly drunk college kids partying in their pajamas. You would also see a lot of kids sleeping in their parents' arms due to the late start time."

Other Wranglers promotions created by Johnson included the Traditional Mullet Hat Night and even a giveaway of orange vests that said, "Don't Shoot...I'm Human!." The barb aimed at Dick Cheney was used during a game on March 17, 2006, a joke on the former Vice President's hunting incident.

In January 2009, the team held the "Rod Blagojevich Prison Uniform Night," parodying the impeachment of the former Governor of Illinois, where both teams wore inmate-like attire — the Wranglers in striped jerseys, the visiting Bakersfield Condors orange jerseys resembling the current Department of Corrections issue. The refs wore blue jerseys resembling prison guards.

Their 2011-2012 home opener was a promotion for "Rapture Day," as this game coincided with the Rapture Prediction of Oakland radio host Harold Camping. On New Year's Day, to parody how the 2012 NHL lockout forced the NHL Winter Classic to be canceled that year, the Wranglers held an "Indoor Winter Classic" that gave a trophy with a chain and a padlock.

Drop The Puck

The Wranglers were fun-loving, yet rough-and-tumble members of the Pacific Division of the Western Conference of the ECHL. The team was founded as an expansion franchise in 2003 following the ECHL's takeover of the West Coast Hockey League.

In May 2014, the team suspended operations for the 2014-2015 ECHL season, allowing it time to secure a new home arena. In 2015, the team withdrew from the ECHL after being unable to find a home arena for the 2015-2016 season.

The Wranglers made two appearances in the Kelly Cup Finals, in 2008 and 2012, and won the Brabham Cup once and the Pacific Division title twice. Former Wranglers who have reached the National Hockey League (NHL) included Brent Krahn, Adam Pardy, Dany Sabourin, Tyson Strachan and Tyler Sloan.

The Wranglers garnered many accolades from the local media, including the Las Vegas Review-Journal naming the Wranglers "Best Local Sports Team" three times (2005, 2006, 2009) and head coach Glen Gulutzan "Best Local Coach" (2007, 2009).

A Rough Patch

On May 29, 2003, in place of owner Charles Davenport, IV, actor Ricky Schroder introduced former Fresno Falcons player/coach Glen Gulutzan as the franchise's first head coach and general manager. Within four months, Gulutzan came to terms with Calgary Flames general manager Darryl Sutter to make the Wranglers the ECHL affiliate of the Flames and Lowell Lock Monsters.

The first two players that Gulutzan signed were brothers and former NHLers Jason and Mike McBain and added veteran ECHL goaltender Marc Magliarditi shortly thereafter. The Wranglers started off their season going 9-1-3 in their first 13 games, and they didn't lose a home game in regulation until a 1-0 loss to the San Diego Gulls on Dec. 27, 2003, going 13-1-1 at home over the stretch. The Wranglers finished their first season with a record of 43-22-7 (93 points), second in the Western Conference's Pacific Division. The Wranglers faced the Idaho Steelheads in the best-of-five Pacific Division Semifinals, and despite overtaking Idaho in the first two games, the Steelheads won the remaining three games on their way to their first Kelly Cup championship.

Entering the 2004-2005 season, Gulutzan and the Wranglers were expected to compete again for the division crown, but instead, the team suffered the worst season in franchise history. Due to the 2004-05 NHL Lockout, local media believed that the team would be stronger, and many Calgary Flames players decided to play for the team's affiliate in Lowell, sending multiple top prospects and former NHLers to the Wranglers' team, including goaltender Sébastien Centomo.

The 2004-2005 Wranglers ended up being more remembered for their lack of discipline as forward Adam

Huxley set a team record for penalty minutes and Centomo became better known for fighting than stopping the puck. Wranglers fans showed their disdain through chants and signs that called for the dismissal of Gulutzan as head coach. The Wranglers finished the season a disappointing 31-33-8 (70 points) and seventh place in the West Division.

Before the 2005-06 season, Wranglers captain Jason McBain announced his retirement, and the team's captaincy was given to his brother, Mike, as the Wranglers looked to shake off the disappointing performance of their sophomore season.

The Wranglers started the season on a rocket pace, losing only four games in the first three months of the season. This included the Wranglers besting their home mark to start a season, as they did not lose at home in regulation until Jan. 3, 2006, 3-2 to the Reading Royals. Before the loss to Reading, the Wranglers had gone 12-0-2 during the time.

One of the most memorable moments during the 2005-2006 season came during the Wranglers' 5-2 win on Nov. 8 as Gulutzan challenged Fresno's head coach Matt Thomas to a fight because Fresno goons Brad Both and Fraser Clair instigated fights with Wranglers rookies Tim Hambly and Lee Green with 11 seconds left in the game.

"The part I remember most about the team was every game I went to, there was a fight," Cordasco recalls. "The league was made of goons. You felt most of these players knew they would never be in the NHL, so they beat up each other every night in the ECHL to earn a paycheck."

The Wranglers ended the season with their best record at 53-13-6 (112 points), only one point behind the Alaska Aces for the West Division title and the Henry Brabham Cup. The 53 wins in 2005-2006 were the most in franchise history, and the 20-win turnaround led to head coach Glen Gulutzan being awarded the John Brophy Award as the league's top coach.

Seeking to improve on a great year, the Wranglers were placed in the National Conference's Pacific Division following a league-wide realignment in 2006. The Wranglers captured the team's first-ever banner, winning the Pacific Division title on April 4, 2007, with a 4-2 victory on the road against the Long Beach Ice Dogs.

The Wranglers finished the 2006-2007 regular season with a 46-12-14 record (106 points) and set the league record for fewest road defeats in a single season with five. The Wranglers also entered the Kelly Cup playoffs on a 13-game winning streak when they took on the 8th-seeded Phoenix Roadrunners in the National Conference quarterfinals.

The Wranglers swept the 'Runners in four games and took on the Idaho Steelheads in the National Conference semifinals. The Wranglers won game one of the series to extend their league-record winning streak to 18 games, tying the 1991 Peoria Rivermen of the International Hockey League for the longest winning streak in professional hockey history. The streak ended in game two, and Idaho eventually took the series in six games on the way to their second Kelly Cup title in four years.

As the Wranglers were set to begin their fifth season in the ECHL, many changes came with it. Mike McKenna left Las Vegas, signing with the Portland Pirates of the AHL, and McBain was not expected to play much of the season before he retired. In turn, Gulutzan signed rookie goaltenders Daniel Manzato and Kevin Lalande, as well as signing twins and former NHLers Chris and Peter Ferraro.

Despite having two untested goaltenders and a team that didn't have a single original Wrangler, the team shot out to 15-2-0 after two months into the season. The Wranglers clinched their second straight Pacific Division crown and National Conference regular season championship on March 26, 2008, with a 3-2 overtime victory on the road against the Utah Grizzlies. The win also made the Wranglers the first team in ECHL history to have three consecutive seasons with at least 100 points.

The Wranglers finished the season 46-13-12 (106 points), good enough for first place in the Pacific Division and the top overall seed in the National Conference playoffs. Right Winger Peter Ferraro would set the team's single-season goal mark with 36. The Wranglers would take on the Stockton Thunder in the National Conference quarterfinals in a series that was tighter than expected.

At the beginning of the series, most of the players that had been called up by Springfield or Edmonton were returned to the team with a high level of experience and pushed the Wranglers to the edge, but Las Vegas was able to recover and take the series in six games. The Wranglers' next opponent would be their heated rival Alaska in the National Conference semifinals. The Wranglers would take the series in five games.

With only four wins away from the Kelly Cup finals, Las Vegas took on the Cinderella 6th-seed Utah Grizzlies. Utah was tough to overcome for Las Vegas, taking the Wranglers to overtime in games two and three before falling to the Wranglers in a four-game sweep as Las Vegas won its first Bruce Taylor Trophy as the

National Conference playoff champions. The Wranglers would meet the 2007-2008 Brabham Cup champ Cincinnati Cyclones in the Kelly Cup finals. The two teams split the first four before Cincinnati stole momentum, defeating the Wranglers in Games 5 and 6.

Following their successful 2007-2008 campaign, the Wranglers were forced to rebuild again as the team was only able to resign nine players from the previous team. The 2008-2009 team was crippled by injuries and inexperienced players. The Wranglers were able to produce a competitive team that finished 34-31-8, mere percentage points behind division champion Ontario.

The Wranglers reached a new level of intensity in their rivalry with the Alaska Aces during the second period of their game on March 25, 2009, in Las Vegas. Alaska's Matt Stefanishion collided with Chris Ferraro, breaking Ferraro's leg and effectively ending his season and possibly his career. Ferraro's twin brother, Peter, became enraged and started a brawl that would involve nine players.

During the melee, Peter Ferraro received a game misconduct penalty for spearing, as did Las Vegas' Tim Spencer for kicking. In the aftermath, the Aces were given a five-minute 5-on-3 power play in which they scored three times before the teams were at even strength. A few days after the game, the ECHL suspended Peter Ferraro for the rest of the regular season and the entirety of the 2009 Kelly Cup Playoffs for his actions during the game and he was released by the team a week later.

The Wranglers entered the playoffs as the second seed in the Pacific Division and took on the third seed Bakersfield Condors in the best-of-seven Pacific Division semifinals. The Wranglers and Condors traded blows in the first four games before Bakersfield took a 3-2 series lead heading back for Games 6 and 7 in Las Vegas. The Wranglers outscored Bakersfield 8-2 in the last two games to take the series.

The Wranglers headed to the Pacific Division finals to face the division's 4th-seed Stockton Thunder. As with the previous series with Bakersfield, the first four games were split by the two teams and Las Vegas took a 3-2 series lead heading back to Las Vegas. Stockton extended the series to a seventh game by defeating the Wranglers 3-1, but the Wranglers finished off the Thunder in Game 7, 5-1.

For the second straight year, the Wranglers reached the National Conference finals, but this time they were to take on the National Conference regular season champion Alaska Aces. Exhausted and injured from two straight seven game series, the Wranglers were unable to retain the Bruce Taylor Trophy, being swept by Alaska in four games.

Gulutzan Leaves, Mougenel Enters

Following an unlikely return to the National Conference finals, Gulutzan left the team to become the head coach of the expansion Texas Stars of the AHL. For the first time in seven years, Wranglers owner Charles Davenport was forced to look for a head coach but stated that Gulutzan's move to the AHL was "long overdue." On June 25, 2009, former Stockton Thunder assistant coach Ryan Mougenel was named the second head coach in franchise history.

On July 15, 2009, the Wranglers announced that they had hired former NHL All-Star Keith Primeau to take over as the team's director of player development as well as being a special assistant to the general manager. Primeau, who played in 15 NHL seasons, ran the Durham Hockey Institute in Toronto with Wranglers head coach and general manager Ryan Mougenel and Keith's brother, Wayne.

The 2009-2010 season was a roller coaster for the Wranglers. Many veteran players left the team as co-owners Davenport and Jonathan Fleisig cut payrolls to save money during the recession. Mougenel went with a youthful team, most of which had little to no professional experience. The team operated with the league's lowest payroll during the 2009-2010 season.

Near the end of 2009, Davenport sold his ownership rights to Fleisig, who assumed full ownership of the team. The team became more consistent following the All-Star break, going 28-18-7 after starting the season 6-12-1 and moving from last place in the National Conference to finish in 2nd place in the Pacific Division. Las Vegas would fall to the Utah Grizzlies in the National Conference Quarterfinals in five games, failing to advance past the first round of the playoffs since their inaugural season.

In mid-April 2010, Felisig reached an agreement with an unidentified buyer who planned to keep the team in Las Vegas. ECHL commissioner Brian McKenna confirmed that the team would return for an eighth season in Las Vegas but couldn't comment further until the transfer of ownership was completed. Mougenel stated that the new owners were "great people" and that "they're real committed to the team." Team president Johnson stated that the team was hoping to make a formal announcement of the transfer by the end of April or the first week of May 2010.

In mid-June 2010, the ECHL Board of Governors gave unanimous approval for the transfer of ownership from Fleisig to Wranglers Hockey LLC led by Gary Jacobs, a real estate developer from San Diego who was managing owner of the Lake Elsinore Storm minor league baseball team.

Mougenel announced in late September 2011 that the Wranglers would play as an independent team (i.e., unaffiliated with any NHL/AHL teams) for the 2011-2012 ECHL season.

Relocation, Suspension, The End

In December 2013, The Orleans Hotel and Casino notified the team that it would not renew their lease for the following season. This prompted the franchise to search for a new venue in the Las Vegas area.

The team announced plans to move to a newly built 3,500-seat facility at the Plaza Hotel & Casino in downtown Las Vegas. However, on May 7, 2014, the team announced that they would not move to the Plaza due to the idea of a rooftop arena becoming unfeasible and an alternative, building the arena in the Plaza's parking lot, being too expensive.

As a result, the Wranglers requested and received a voluntary suspension of operations from the ECHL for the 2014-2015 season. The team planned to seek a new permanent venue and returned to play in the 2015-2016 season.

On Jan. 30, 2015, it was announced via Facebook that the Wranglers would cease operations after not being able to find a suitable home within a reasonable timeframe to submit to the board of governors of the ECHL. Soon after, Las Vegas was awarded a National Hockey League franchise.

Former Wranglers who reached the National Hockey League (NHL) include Brent Krahn, Adam Pardy, Dany Sabourin, Tyson Strachan and Tyler Sloan.

Chris Gawlik, Vegas Hockey Now/Locked On Golden Knights podcaster who attended many Wranglers games, said, "The Wranglers planted strong hockey roots in Las Vegas, and it's amazing seeing what those roots have become. Las Vegas is a growing hockey city, and much credit can go to the Wranglers."

Good while it lasted.

Team Logo

The Wranglers' first logo featured a cowboy riding a bull and holding a hockey stick with Las Vegas Wranglers script below the bull. The cowboy and bull are both black and white and are outlined in silver. The script consists of "Las Vegas" in silver cursive, while "Wranglers" is in white with silver accents. Prior to the WCHL-ECHL merger, the Wranglers logo was an outline of a cowboy's face streaking to the left with a black cowboy hat and red and yellow outlines. A script underneath the logo featured "Las Vegas" in black above "Wranglers" in yellow with a red outline.

On July 5, 2012, the Wranglers unveiled their new identity package; the primary logo featured a cowboy's head inside a shield with a goalie mask over his face. The cowboy hat is black and gray, with the mask white and gray, and the shield in two shades of red and outlined in black. Beneath the cowboy is a red eight-pointed star, and on either side of him is a white "LV" and "NV," representing the city and state's abbreviation.

Mascot

The Wranglers' mascot was "The Duke," a 7-foot-3-inch (2.21 m) green bull that was based on the Philly Phanatic and was the team's mascot since its inaugural season in 2003. The Duke kept the crowd excited, signed autographs, and participated in entertainment during intermissions and player introductions at the beginning of the game.

The Duke also was a regular at other events around the city, including races at the Las Vegas Motor Speedway, also making appearances with players at local elementary schools. The Duke attended three ECHL All-Star Games as the league's favorite mascot.

Wranglers' mascot, The Duke.

2006-2007 Logo

Team Information

Las Vegas Wranglers ECHL 2003-2015

Record 11 Seasons   (GP-W-L-T-OTL)

      793-425-279-0 (0.592)

Franchise History: Expansion franchise for 2003-2004.

Las Vegas Wranglers « (2003-2015)

Withdrew from the league following the 2014-2015 season.

Parent Teams

San Antonio Rampage (2009-2011) [AHL]

Quad City Flames (2007-2009) [AHL]

Omaha Ak-Sar-Ben Knights (2005-2007) [AHL]

Lowell Lock Monsters (2004-2005) [AHL]

Wranglers Yearly Standings

| Season | Team | League | Division | | GP | W | L | T | OTL | SOL | Pts | Pct | GF |
GA	PIM	Atten.	Coach	Result									
2003-04	Las Vegas Wranglers	ECHL	Pacific	72	43	22	0	0	7	93	0.646	227	
186	1605	4981	Glen Gulutzan	Lost in round 1									
2004-05	Las Vegas Wranglers	ECHL	West	72	31	33	0	3	5	70	0.486	201	
199	1666	5193	Glen Gulutzan	Out of Playoffs									
2005-06	Las Vegas Wranglers	ECHL	West	72	53	13	0	4	2	112	0.778	267	
176	1513	5531	Glen Gulutzan	Lost in round 3									
2006-07	Las Vegas Wranglers	ECHL	Pacific	72	46	12	0	6	8	106	0.736	231	
187	1374	5075	Glen Gulutzan	Lost in round 3									
2007-08	Las Vegas Wranglers	ECHL	Pacific	72	47	13	0	5	7	106	0.736	244	
179	1440	4970	Glen Gulutzan	Lost in Finals									
2008-09	Las Vegas Wranglers	ECHL	Pacific	73	34	31	0	2	6	76	0.521	208	
195	1622	4621	Glen Gulutzan	Lost in round 3									
2009-10	Las Vegas Wranglers	ECHL	Pacific	72	34	30	0	4	4	76	0.528	234	
257	1421	4350	Ryan Mougenel	Lost in round 1									
2010-11	Las Vegas Wranglers	ECHL	Pacific	72	38	29	0	3	2	81	0.563	216	
203	1006	3940	Ryan Mougenel	Lost in round 1									
2011-12	Las Vegas Wranglers	ECHL	Pacific	72	42	22	0	1	7	92	0.639	235	
198	1058	4339	Ryan Mougenel	Lost in Finals									
2012-13	Las Vegas Wranglers	ECHL	Pacific	72	37	30	0	2	3	79	0.549	196	
192	1206	4561	Ryan Mougenel	Lost in round 1									
2013-14	Las Vegas Wranglers	ECHL	Pacific	72	20	44	0	4	4	48	0.333	174	
248	1128	4581	Mike Madill	Lost in round 1									

Chapter 9
Building a Fan Base

SNMHA
(Southern Nevada Minor League Hockey Association)

The explosion of youth hockey in Las Vegas has grown from a few kids skating on the International Ice Palace around chairs in the late 1960s to thousands of youngsters playing from Summerlin to Henderson. Ice surfaces in the Valley can no longer accommodate the demand for games and practice time.

Indeed, the story of the Southern Nevada Minor Hockey Association (SNMHA) encapsulates the essence of community-driven efforts that shaped today's broader hockey landscape. With desert sands as its backdrop, Las Vegas may not be the first place one would associate with ice hockey. Yet, with the determination of individuals and the cohesive unity of a community, what seemed unlikely became reality.

The first known hockey instruction came without pay or organized practices back in 1968.

"We taught so many kids how to skate," Gamblers player Bill Briski said. "We'd get a folding chair out there and let them push it around the ice," Gamblers alum Brian Bulmer recalled.

Bulmer estimates that over the years, he and his teammates taught a few hundred kids in Las Vegas how to skate.

"It was more like a community-type thing," Briski said. "And the parents would be in there, and that would help our thing, too. Get the parents and the kids interested in our game."

First Structured Program

In many ways, the journey of the SNMHA is a testament to the adage that "it takes a village." It wasn't just about bringing hockey to a desert; it was about building a community and nurturing the dreams of countless young players. The grassroots movement in Las Vegas, spearheaded by these devoted individuals, has surely paved the way for the region's next generation of ice hockey enthusiasts.

Hockey coach and former Flint Generals VP Bob Lawson was the first to organize youth hockey. His arrival came in 1993, and he was armed with his extensive experience from the Greater Flint Hockey Association (GFHA), Flint, MI. His efforts and the efforts of his father were a turning point for amateur hockey in Southern Nevada.

"It's fascinating how the interwoven stories of

Bob Lawson

individuals can influence the trajectory of an entire sporting community," Lawson said.

The connection between Lawson, Gale Cronk (GFHA founder/director), and Ken Morrow, whose legacies are rooted in GFHA, illustrates the powerful ripple effect of knowledge and passion.

It is often said that transplanting a successful model from one region to another requires more than just replication; it requires adaptation. With its diverse challenges, Las Vegas needed a model that respected its singularities but also drew from the well-estalished methods of the GFHA. The synergy of adopting tried-and-true methodologies while tailoring them to local needs was instrumental in the successes of SNMHA programs and the Henderson Roller Hockey Youth program.

The contribution of Dale Lewis, a local Las Vegan and elected President of the SNMHA's leadership in the formative years, cannot be understated. His dedication, combined with the expertise of Lawson and the framework of GFHA, created an environment where young talents could flourish.

And flourish it did during the next 15 to 20 years, Las Vegas would play host to the fastest growing youth hockey movement in the country on skates, both ice and roller.

Morrow, having an illustrious career that included 4 Stanley Cup Rings and being part of the 'Miracle on Ice' team, added an extra layer of inspiration to the impact Ken made on the development of the roller hockey youth programs spawned from the Las Vegas Flash RHI (Roller Hockey International) team during the 93-94 season.

Rob Pallin, formerly an assistant coach with the Las Vegas Wranglers, also has helped develop players in the city's youth hockey program, including the Minnesota Wild's Jason Zucker, along with minor leaguers Cory Ward and Gage Quinney.

Young Rising Stars: The first Las Vegas "A" level travel youth hockey team for the 1994-1995 season with Coach Bob Lawson and son Blake Lawson. The team traveled outside Nevada for games and tournaments and had practices with the Aces.

He said he has no doubt the NHL will work in Las Vegas.

"It's an exciting time for the sport," Pallin said. "I give Mr. Foley credit for his willingness to fight through the challenges, be patient, and stay with it until the end. There's a great fan base here, and I have no doubt they'll support the NHL."

Overcoming Obstacles

With time, persistence and a vision, obstacles have a way of becoming gateways to opportunities.

Las Vegas's reputation, while globally recognized for its alluring casinos, was ironically the very reason it struggled to embrace the world of professional sports. The potential conflicts between sports gaming and the integrity of professional sports were palpable. Integrity, fairness, and impartiality are the cornerstones of any sporting event, and the apprehension of these being compromised in a city synonymous with gambling was significant.

But challenges have a way of incubating innovation. Instead of viewing sports gaming as a hurdle, some visionary individuals and organizations began to see it as a unique advantage – a distinctive feature that no other city could offer. The conversation started shifting from "Can we introduce professional sports in a gaming city?" to "How can we seamlessly integrate sports gaming with professional sports to create a new experience?"

Legal Loophole

As the broader sports industry began to evolve, so did the acceptance of sports gaming. The advent of fantasy leagues and legalized betting in various parts of the world significantly destigmatized the association between sports and betting.

While working at Caesars Palace, PR Coordinator Richard Gubbe found a way to publicize the Caesars Sports Book without having to pay a dime by giving it to any newspaper from coast to coast.

"Prior to the first outdoor hockey game in 1991, I discovered a loophole in the 1961 federal Wire Act. I asked myself why sports betting gurus like Jim Feist and Lem Banker had sports betting lines they sold to daily newspapers coast to coast, but a casino never did," Gubbe said.

The Wire Act is a United States law prohibiting the operation of certain types of betting businesses in the United States. It begins with the text:

"Whoever being engaged in the business of betting or wagering knowingly uses a wire communication facility for the transmission in interstate or foreign commerce of bets or wagers or information assisting in the placing of bets or wagers on any sporting event or contest, or for the transmission of a wire communication which entitles the recipient to receive money or credit as a result of bets or wagers, or for information assisting in the placing of bets or wagers, shall be fined under this title or imprisoned not more than two years, or both."

"After reading it, I went to VP Don Guglielmino and pointed out that Fax machines don't use wires," Gubbe recalled. "He took it to the legal department they said to run with it. Every morning, I would take the latest lines from the sportsbook and send them to various newspapers across the country. Sports betting websites do the same thing now, and they also are circumventing the Wire Act."

Several legal opinions and rulings have discussed whether forms of gambling other than sports betting fall within the Act's scope, but no laws have yet been enacted.

When it came to Las Vegas, the key was establishing rigorous regulatory frameworks. By ensuring transparency in betting processes, deploying technology for monitoring, and running awareness campaigns about responsible gambling, the city began to slowly earn the trust of the Big Four sports leagues.

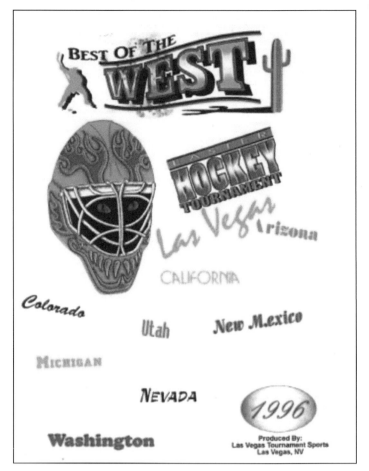

The Bright Future

The introduction of professional teams was a watershed moment for Las Vegas. It not only reshaped its identity but also created a ripple effect, breathing life into ancillary sectors. The absence of youth programs and merchandising had created a latent demand, and once the professional teams set foot, these sectors experienced explosive growth.

Quickly, Las Vegas's rinks, courts, and fields buzzed with young aspirants dreaming of making it big. Merchandisers latched on to this enthusiasm, filling shops with jerseys, equipment and memorabilia.

The story of Las Vegas's foray into professional sports is a testament to the city's indefatigable spirit. It reaffirms that when a community comes together, driven by a shared passion and guided by visionary leadership, even the harshest of deserts can echo with the cheers of packed stadiums.

With the Las Vegas Aces starting to create a following, along with the RHI Flash, and the Las Vegas Thunder in the 93-94 seasons, advanced-level youth programs and hockey events would inevitably follow.

By the 1995-1996 season, ice hockey and roller hockey had significant youth hockey development happening. And the Lawson family was right in the middle. Lawson had returned to Michigan as the VP of Marketing for the Flint Generals, Colonial Hockey League, joining his buddy and former NHLer Robbie

Nichols GM/head coach, who had just finished his tenure with the San Diego Gulls in the IHL, and the San Diego Barracudas in the RHI. Nichols and Lawson set several records that season with the 1995-1996 Generals: Attendance, Win/Loss %, Sponsorship sales, and a Colonial Cup title, to name a few.

With Bob Lawson back in Michigan, his father, Robert Lawson Jr., stepped in, and with his son Bob's Media and Public Relations right hand, Richard Gubbe, created "Las Vegas Tournament Sports." In 1995, LVTS hosted the 1995 First Annual "National In-Line Hockey Championships", and in the 1996 season created the first "Best of the West" ice hockey tournament, hosting 60 youth hockey teams playing over 200 games start to finish. Teams from as far east as New York and Florida, as well as Bob Lawson's youth team with his son, Blake, a Squirt I captain with the IMA Knights team from Flint.

Over the next 3 years, LVTS grew the "Best of the West" to over 300 teams, making it one of the largest Youth Hockey Tournaments in the country.

The biggest annual adult fantasy hockey came from the Great One himself. Wayne Gretzky held seven camps in Las Vegas from 2010 to 2017.

As the Las Vegas Golden Knights continue to shine in the NHL, they stand on the shoulders of these grassroots giants who fostered a love for the game in the heart of the desert.

Chapter 10
Bruckheimer Fans on Shot at Vegas Franchise

The Golden Knights almost never existed. Almost. If it weren't for one of the most devastating recessions of all time, Hollywood movie and TV mogul Jerry Bruckheimer was part of an investment group that had the inside track at bringing an NHL franchise to Las Vegas.

Jerry Bruckheimer

Bruckheimer was named as one of the investors in a plan to team with Harrah's, which bought Caesars Palace, to beat Bill Foley to the punch in 2007. Las Vegas had been rumored to be the leading choice by the National Hockey League (NHL) to own an expansion hockey team that would play on the Strip. Then came the market crash.

Bruckheimer admitted to his attempt, and despite the recession, he said his group remained interested. He said, "But it's a waiting game until the economy recovers, Las Vegas is a growing city, a big city. It has travelers from all over the world who are hockey fans, and I think this city could use a professional sports team."

Bruckheimer had a lot of money behind him. Bruckheimer was part of an investment group that also included Tim Leiweke (Oak View Group) and David Bonderman (minority owner of the NBA's Boston Celtics).

"I played hockey when I was a little kid, poorly, and started playing again when I got to California, [but] I always dreamt about being part of professional sports," Bruckheimer said. "So, I met an individual named Harry Sloan, a big financial wizard, and we started this quest to try to buy or develop a hockey team, a National Hockey League team. He eventually introduced me to a man named David Bonderman, who's another financial wizard. He's like the Michael Jordan of finances."

The three men were prepared to invest in an expansion team for Las Vegas in 2007, pending completion of an arena project located on Koval Lane behind then Bally's and Paris Las Vegas. Tim Leiweke, another member of the group, had partnered with Harrah's Entertainment Inc. to build the arena, which was to cost an estimated $500 million and seat 22,000.

When Harrah's and entertainment giant AEG announced the Las Vegas plans in August 2007 for a 20,000-seat arena to be built behind Bally's, the date given for the arena opening was proposed for 2010.

Leiweke was no stranger to the NHL. He was governor of the Los Angeles Kings from 1996 to 2013 when he was president of Anschutz Entertainment Group. From 2013 to 2015, he was president of the Toronto Maple Leafs when he was with Maple Leaf Sports and Entertainment.

Longtime entertainment columnist Norm Clark reported as late as June 23, 2010, in the Las Vegas Review-Journal, "The recession hasn't dampened his (Bruckheimer's) interest in owning an NHL team in Las Vegas."

Bonderman, an investment banker whose worth was estimated by Forbes magazine to be $2.5 billion more than five years ago, and Bruckheimer, whose worth was then estimated at $900 million, shifted their focus to a potential Seattle franchise.

"We have never announced a deal and not built," Leiweke said at the Aug. 23, 2007, news conference announcing the project. "We'll save our bluffing for the tables downstairs."

Then the Great Recession hit in 2008, and the project was dead by late 2010.

"The arena was the biggest hurdle to clear," said veteran sportswriter Steve Carp. "Then Caesars (Harrah's) backed out. His nut would have been well over $1 billion without them."

Years later, that project was gobbled up by Bill Foley's group. Bruckheimer was determined to be an owner in the NHL. He had a close relationship with the NHL and was the league's leading candidate to get the next franchise. He was named as one of the investors of a proposed Seattle-based NHL expansion team, whose application was submitted in early 2018.

The NHL Board of Governors voted to approve the team, named the Seattle Kraken, on Dec. 4, 2018, which started to play in the 2021-22 season.

"I stumbled around and tried to buy a number of teams, but we eventually, through Tim Leiweke, figured out a way to take the Key Arena in Seattle and turn it into a brand-new arena and convince the city, and then NHL, to build the arena and then give us an expansion team."

"He turned Key Arena into an NHL facility," Carp said. "Seattle was going to be the next city with NHL and the Kraken did all the right things. If they hadn't had the recession, they would have built an arena in Vegas. I think it worked out better by waiting."

The Kraken became the first professional hockey team to play in Seattle since the Seattle Totems of the Western Hockey League played their last game in 1975.

Chapter 11
Frozen Fury Hits Vegas

The first NHL exhibition game played in Las Vegas also was the first outdoor game in the league's history at a rink set up outside Caesars Palace. A large crowd saw the Kings defeat the New York Rangers 5-2 on Sept. 28, 1991. The air temperature was 85 °F (29 °C) during the game. The game served as a predecessor to the Ice Breaker game indoors at the Thomas & Mack on Sept. 26, 1996, sponsored by Caesars.

The MGM, with Dennis Finfrock and Darren Libonati, met the Los Angeles Kings officials to keep the pro exhibition games going and created Frozen Fury. The first Frozen Fury pre-season game between the Los Angeles Kings and the Colorado Avalanche was held in 1997. From 1997 to 2015, these games were played at MGM Grand Garden Arena.

The 15th Frozen Fury was originally supposed to take place on Sept. 29, 2012, but was canceled due to the NHL lockout. It resumed Sept. 27-28, 2013, with the New York Rangers making their debut in the series.

In 2016, two contests were played at T-Mobile Arena. The 2016 games were the last of the original tradition due to the launch of the Vegas Golden Knights in the 2017-2018 season.

The series has continued with the Vegas Golden Knights in Salt Lake City since 2021. The current Frozen Fury series was launched at Vivint Arena in Salt Lake City between the Kings and the Golden Knights.

The NHL Winter Classic, the annual regular season outdoor game held on New Year's Day, began in 2008 and continues each year.

Frozen Fury Year By Year

Frozen Fury I
Sept. 20, 1997 Los Angeles Kings 4, Colorado Avalanche 3 (OT)
Frozen Fury II
Sept. 19, 1998 Los Angeles Kings 3, Colorado Avalanche 2
Sept. 20, 1998 Colorado Avalanche 5, Los Angeles Kings 4
Frozen Fury III
Sept. 11, 1999 Los Angeles Kings 4, Phoenix Coyotes 0
Frozen Fury IV
Sept. 30, 2000 Colorado Avalanche 5, Los Angeles Kings 4
Frozen Fury V
Sept. 22, 2001 Los Angeles Kings 4, San Jose Sharks 3

Frozen Fury VI
Oct. 5, 2002 Los Angeles Kings 6, Colorado Avalanche 5
Frozen Fury VII
Sept. 23, 2003 Los Angeles Kings 3, Colorado Avalanche 1
Frozen Fury VIII
Sept. 24, 2005 Colorado Avalanche 2, Los Angeles Kings 1 (OT)
Frozen Fury IX
Sept. 23, 2006 Los Angeles Kings 3, Colorado Avalance 2
Frozen Fury X
Sept. 22, 2007 Los Angeles Kings 3, Colorado Avalanche 2 (SO)
Frozen Fury XI
Sept. 27, 2008 Colorado Avalanche 4, Los Angeles Kings 3 (SO)
Frozen Fury XII
Sept. 26, 2009, Los Angeles 5, Colorado Avalanche 3
Frozen Fury XIII
Oct. 2, 2010 Los Angeles Kings 3, Colorado Avalanche 2
Frozen Fury XIV
Oct. 1, 2011 Colorado Avalanche 4, Los Angeles Kings 1
Frozen Fury XV
Sept. 27, 2013, Los Angeles Kings 4, New York Rangers 1
Sept. 28, 2013 Colorado Avalanche 3, Los Angeles Kings 2
Frozen Fury XVI
Oct. 4, 2014, Colorado Avalanche 3, Los Angeles Kings 2, SO
Frozen Fury XVII
Oct. 3, 2015 Los Angeles Kings 4, Colorado Avalanche 0
Frozen Fury XVIII
Oct. 7, 2016 Dallas Stars 6, Los Angeles Kings 3
Oct. 8, 2016 Colorado Avalanche 2, Los Angeles Kings 1 (OT)
Frozen Fury SLC I
Sept. 30, 2021 Los Angeles Kings 3, Vegas Golden Knights 1
Frozen Fury SLC II
Oct. 6, 2022 Vegas Golden Knights 6, Los Angeles Kings 4

Chapter 12
Failed & Defunct Franchises in Las Vegas

Las Vegas has built a reputation for being where fledgling sports franchises go to die. Only the Las Vegas Stars baseball club and its spinoffs have survived, mainly due to the support of Major League Baseball, casinos and a strong marketing approach. For all others, the product was poorly run or poorly promoted, or ownership was too cheap to invest any long-lasting funds into a team or the product wasn't well received by the community. The owners thought just because the team was in Vegas, people would flock to their games. Instead, empty seats were often the norm. Here are all the franchises that floundered before the Vegas Golden Knights came to town to post sellouts instead of unused tickets.

Las Vegas Aces

The Las Vegas Aces began as a Senior Professional hockey team based in Las Vegas during the 1992-1993 season under GM Maurice Slepica and Player Coach Bob Campbell. After playing a season of exhibition games hosting teams from around the U.S., the team, under new GM/ Head Coach Robert Lawson, joined the PSHL (Pacific Southwest Hockey League) for the 1993-1994 schedule. The team's home arena was based in the Santa Fe Resort and Casino. The Aces were members of the semi-pro PSHL for two seasons and returned to exhibition play following the 1994-1995 season. The 1993-1994 season was comprised of notable collegiate hockey players from some of the best hockey teams in the country. Many of these players also were rostered on the new RHI expansion Las Vegas Flash in the 1993 campaign under Head Coach Kenny Morrow.

The Aces, confirmed as the first true professional hockey team in Las Vegas, was also the first team to actually market season and individual tickets on a regular schedule. During the 1993-1994 season, most of the games played to sell-out attendance in the Santa Fe Arena.

During the 1994-1995 season, the roster was headlined by Larry Melnyk, a Stanley Cup-winning defenseman with the Edmonton Oilers who played in the NHL throughout the 1980s with Edmonton, the Boston Bruins, New York Rangers and Vancouver Canucks. After retiring in 1990, Melnyk made a comeback attempt with the Aces, but he and the team only lasted one more season in 1994-1995.

Las Vegas Americans

The Las Vegas Americans were a soccer team based out of Las Vegas that played in the original Major Indoor Soccer League. Before Las Vegas, the team had operated as the Memphis Americans. They only played in Las Vegas during the 1984-1985 season and lost in the first round of the playoffs that year. The Las Vegas Americans finished their only season in the league with a 30-18 record, earning them second place in the Western Division of the league. Their home arena was Thomas & Mack Center, and their average attendance was 6,337. The Americans were expelled from the Major Indoor Soccer League on July 17, 1985, when the MISL board of directors voted to terminate the franchise due to financial troubles.

Las Vegas Blackjacks RFC

The Las Vegas Blackjacks Rugby Football Club (Las Vegas Blackjacks RFC) was a rugby union team based in Las Vegas. They were members of the Southern California Rugby Football Union and competed in the Senior Men's 1st (Red) Division of USA Rugby. The Las Vegas Rugby Club was established in 1976 following a newspaper advertisement to recruit players for a local rugby club. The Blackjacks finished in fourth place at the USA Rugby Nationals - Division I Tournament and won their first SCRFU Regular Season title in 2008. The Blackjacks won the regular season again in 2009 and made it to the National Final, where they lost to the Gentlemen of Aspen. Redemption was found in 2010 as the boys claimed the nation's top prize with a win in the national final against Belmont Shore.

In 2010, LVRC signed a player development agreement with Top 14 side Montpellier Hérault RC. The agreement with Montpellier had the French side sending young players to play with LVRC during France's offseason while allowing amateur players with the Blackjacks the opportunity to play top-level professional rugby. The team folded after the 2011 season.

Las Vegas Coyotes

The Las Vegas Coyotes were an inline hockey team that never competed in Roller Hockey International. The team was founded as the Atlanta Fire Ants in 1994 and had a two-season stint in Oklahoma City before the team relocated to Las Vegas. The team folded after the 1999 season. The Coyotes were the second attempt to field a team in the Las Vegas Valley; the Coyotes predecessor, the Flash, played one season in the RHI.

Las Vegas Dealers

The Las Vegas Dealers were one of seven founding teams in the Western Basketball Association in 1978. The Dealers proved to be the league's shakiest franchise and barely made it through the season. Dealers founders James Speed and his wife, Sylvia, came to ownership through unusual – and sad – circumstances. A 6' 7", James Speed was a prized recruit for the University of Iowa basketball program in 1970. Before he ever took the floor for the Hawkeyes, complications from routine medical procedures left him permanently blind in both eyes. Speed later used part of his $750,000 malpractice judgment to buy the Dealers.

Las Vegas Dustdevils

The Las Vegas Dustdevils were an indoor soccer team based out of Las Vegas that played in the Continental Indoor Soccer League (CISL). The team won the league championship in 1994 but folded after their second season.

Las Vegas Flash

The Las Vegas Flash was an inline hockey team that existed for one season in 1994. The Flash was a part of Roller Hockey International. The team's home games were played at the Thomas & Mack Center and featured many pro hockey players, past and current. The team was coached by former NHL and 1980 Olympics star Kenny Morrow. The GM was Bob Lawson and Richard Gubbe was the PR Director. They teamed up again as co-authors for *Vegas Hockey, Vegas Strong.*

Strong authors Bob Lawson, and Richard Gubbe was the PR Director.

The franchise was previously known as the Utah Rollerbees (1993). The team played in the Salt Palace II in Salt Lake City. That franchise was replaced by the Utah Sun Dogs (1997-1999), then replaced by the Las Vegas Coyotes in 1999.

The Flash set the RHI league record for opening night attendance at the home rink in the Thomas & Mack arena. The team was also one of the most successful startups in Las Vegas Sports for purchased ticket sales. The Flash only lasted for the one season due to lack of ownership support.

Las Vegas Gamblers

The Las Vegas Gamblers, aka Nevada Gamblers, began as a senior amateur team, but grew into a semi-pro squad that played in the California-Nevada Hockey League (although rumors persist that most of these players were unpaid, which would negate its semi-pro moniker).

That same league later morphed into the Pacific Southwest Hockey League, and then into the West Coast Hockey League. An unaffiliated version of the team played on before disbanding in the mid-1990s. Before it ceased to exist, this league, throughout all its modifications, housed two separate Las Vegas franchises, as well as three in Reno (the Gamblers, Renegades, and an early version of the Aces).

Las Vegas Locos

The Las Vegas Locomotives (called the Locos for short) were a professional American football team based in Las Vegas that played in the United Football League. The team played their home games at Sam Boyd Stadium, home field for the University of Nevada, Las Vegas. Jim Fassel was the franchise's head coach, president and general manager.T he Locomotives appeared in all three UFL Championship Games, winning both the 2009 and 2010 titles. The Locos also were the last of the four charter UFL franchises to remain in their original home city, to retain their original head coach, and to have played all their home games at the same venue.

Las Vegas was one of the first markets to be considered for a UFL team. When the league released its tentative list of six markets for their inaugural season in early 2008, it included Las Vegas, Los Angeles, New York, Hartford, Orlando, and San Francisco. When the league contracted to four teams prior to the start of the 2009 season, Las Vegas merged with Los Angeles, while New York merged with Hartford. Eventually, despite New York and Los Angeles being the larger markets, Las Vegas and Hartford were given sole rights to the teams, and Las Vegas never played a game in the Los Angeles metro area.

Las Vegas was awarded a franchise for the inaugural season of the UFL in 2009. The team named Fassel as head coach. Fassel led his team to a 4-2 record in his first season. In the 2009 UFL Championship Game, the Locos defeated the then-undefeated Florida Tuskers to become the league's first champions.

Las Vegas Outlaws Football

The Las Vegas Outlaws were an American football team in the XFL. They played in the Western Division with the Los Angeles Xtreme, San Francisco Demons and Memphis Maniax. They played their home games at Sam Boyd Stadium. On February 3, 2001, The Outlaws hosted the first nationally televised XFL game on NBC against the New York/New Jersey Hitmen.

Before the 2001 season began, there already was a question if Las Vegas could support a professional sports team due to past failed attempts. The Outlaws were sponsored by Cox Communications, New York-New York Hotel & Casino, Station Casinos, PacifiCare Health Systems and Findlay Toyota. Just like the Posse (and the later Locomotives), the Outlaws had a difficult time selling tickets. For the home opener against the Hitmen 13,700 tickets were sold for a stadium that seats 36,000. There were only 7,000 estimated season ticket holders. Compared to the rest of the league, the Outlaws' attendance was about 22,000 fans per game. They were one of two teams (the league-leading San Francisco Demons being the other) to consistently play in a stadium that was more than half-full. The league-leading defense, led by Defensive Coordinator Mark Criner, was nicknamed "The Dealers of Doom."

Among the team's players was the XFL's most well-known, Rod Smart (later with the National Football League's Philadelphia Eagles, Carolina Panthers and the Oakland Raiders), who went by the nickname "He Hate Me," which appeared on the back of his jersey. (He was originally going to put "They Hate Me," but there wasn't enough room). Coached by former Boise State and Scottish Claymores head coach Jim Criner, the Outlaws competed in the XFL's only season, held in the spring of 2001. The team encouraged their fans to come up with a nickname. They selected the "Dealers of Doom Defense." After a strong start, the Outlaws suffered repeated injuries to their quarterbacks (by the midpoint of the season, they were on their fourth-string quarterback) and lost their last three games to finish in last place in the division with a record of 4-6-0, just one game out of a playoff spot.

Despite having a two-year contract, NBC announced shortly after the season that it was getting out, as the season's later games had garnered the lowest ratings for a major American television network since the Nielsen ratings had begun tracking them, and the league folded shortly afterward.

The team was the centerpiece of the 2003 book about the XFL, "Long Bomb: How the XFL Became TV's Biggest Fiasco." It was written by Brett Forrest of Details magazine.

Las Vegas Ice Dice

The Ice Dice didn't have the most memorable stay on the hockey scene, joining the North American League in 1995, but disbanding before they played a game. The most memorable aspect of this team was that a hockey team was called the "Ice Dice."

Las Vegas Neon

The brief, 30-day lifespan of the Las Vegas Neon was an embarrassing footnote in the long history of World TeamTennis. The niche co-ed tennis league lost its oldest franchise in February 2014 when the Sacramento Capitals moved to Las Vegas after 28 seasons in Northern California. The Capitals endured nearly three decades in the turbulent, high-turnover league. The team's last few seasons were anything but stable, with persistent ownership and financial and venue problems. The team's last benefactor in Sacramento was Deepal Wannakuwatte, a medical supply company owner who took over the league's Capitals in 2011. Wannakuwatte announced the move to Las Vegas on February 4, 2014, citing the Capitals stadium woes as the primary reason for the move. The Capitals played the 2013 season in a shopping mall parking lot. Barely three weeks after announcing the move to Vegas, Deepal Wannakuwatte was arrested on charges of running a decade-long $150 million Ponzi scheme. World TeamTennis revoked and disbanded the Las Vegas Neon on March 5th, 2014. Wannakuwatte pleaded guilty to fraud charges in May 2014 and was sentenced to 20 years in prison in 2014.

Las Vegas Posse

The Las Vegas Posse was a Canadian Football League (CFL) team, that played at the Sam Boyd Silver Bowl in the league's 1994 season as part of the CFL's short-lived American expansion. Lasting only one season, the Posse was one of the least successful teams in CFL history, both on the field and off.

The Posse had notable football talents such as KR Tamarick Vanover, RB Jon Volpe, LB Greg Battle, LB Shonte Peoples, DB/QB Darian Hagan and K Carlos Huerta, and had rookie quarterback Anthony Calvillo.

The franchise also had an experienced coaching staff with Head Coach Ron Meyer, who had previous coaching experiences with UNLV and in the NFL, and also had future Winnipeg Blue Bombers coach Jeff Reinebold as one of their assistant coaches. Huerta won the Jackie Parker Trophy as the Most Outstanding Rookie of the West Division that year.

The Posse started with wins over the Sacramento Gold Miners and Saskatchewan Roughriders, but things quickly went downhill, in part due to a lack of familiarity with the Canadian game. For instance, during a game against the BC Lions, Vanover signaled for a fair catch, not knowing that there was no fair catch in Canadian football, with the ball rolling into the Posse end zone, which the Lions promptly recovered for a touchdown. Players also openly complained about the apathy of their coaches and teammates.

The Posse finished the season 5-13, finishing last in the West Division and next-to-last in the CFL.

Las Vegas Quicksilver, the Las Vegas Quicksilvers

The Las Vegas Quicksilvers were an American soccer team that competed in the North American Soccer League (NASL) during the 1977 season. The team played their home games at Las Vegas Stadium. After the 1977 season, the team relocated to San Diego and became the San Diego Sockers. Eusébio, considered by many to be one of the greatest players of all time, played 17 matches and scored two goals for the Quicksilvers.

Las Vegas Rollers WTT

World TeamTennis, which was founded by tennis legend Billie Jean King, has been in existence since 1974. WTT is one of five active U.S. pro sports leagues that has been in operation for more than 40 years. Teams are co-ed and matches are played in men's and women's singles, men's and women's doubles and mixed doubles. The Rollers marked WTT's second attempt to establish a team in Las Vegas. In 2014, the league's plans for a team known as the Las Vegas Neon were scuttled when team owner Deepal Wannakuwatte was revealed to be the mastermind of a $150 million Ponzi scheme. The Neon never played a match.

In the league record books, the Rollers were a two-year entry in World TeamTennis. But in reality, the Vegas Rollers were merely tourists, whose entire residency at the Orleans Arena consisted of 7 matches crammed into an 11-day stretch between July 20 and July 30, 2019. The 2019 Rollers team finished 6-8 and failed to qualify for WTT's postseason tournament at Orleans Arena.

What would have been the Rollers' second season in 2020 was disrupted by the COVID-19 pandemic. The entire 2020 World TeamTennis season was conducted at The Greenbrier luxury resort in West Virginia, primarily for the benefit of a video streaming audience and cable viewers on the CBS Sports Network. The Rollers took part in the season, but no operations took place in Nevada.

WTT introduced professional team tennis to the world in 1974. The new team in Las Vegas, as well as the new team in Orlando, Fla., joined the league's existing franchises - New York Empire, Orange County Breakers, Philadelphia Freedoms, San Diego Aviators, Springfield Lasers and Washington Kastles - for play in July 2019. The WTT 2019 season consisted of 59 regular season matches, including seven home matches and seven away matches for each team between July 14-31. The Orleans Arena hosted the home matches for the Rollers in addition to the league's Semifinals on Friday, Aug. 2 and the WTT Finals on Saturday, Aug. 3.

In May 2021, World TeamTennis announced that its 2021 schedule, set for November, would once again be held in a single location. A shrunken lineup of five teams would compete at the Indian Wells Tennis Garden in California. No mention of the Rollers or the other non-participating franchises was made in the announcement, and they appear to be defunct.

Las Vegas Seagulls

The Las Vegas Seagulls was an American soccer club based in Whitney, Nevada, that was a member of the American Soccer League. The club played one season in 1979.

Las Vegas Silver Streaks basketball team

The Las Vegas Silver Streaks were a professional basketball franchise based in Las Vegas from 1988-1990. The team played its inaugural seasons in the World Basketball League before folding. The Silver Streaks won the first World Basketball League championship in 1988, defeating the Chicago Express 102-95 in the title game. They were one of only three teams to ever win a WBL championship. Creation of a league franchise team for Las Vegas was facilitated by former Oakland A's executive Fred Kuenzi. He stayed on and served as a general manager and promotions director for season 1.The Silver Streaks played its home games at the Thomas & Mack Center. Former UNLV stars Freddie Banks, Anthony Jones and Mark Wade played for the club.

Las Vegas Stallions

Las Vegas Stallions were an American soccer club. They played in the National Premier Soccer League. They were one of the main soccer clubs in Las Vegas, Nevada. Piggott Memorial Stadium was their venue. It had a capacity of 3,000 people. The Las Vegas Stallions withdrew from the NPSL and folded in 2014.

Las Vegas Stars (Basketball)

The Las Vegas Stars club was a professional basketball team in the International Basketball League. The inaugural head coach was George Tarkanian, son of famed coach Jerry Tarkanian. The CEO/General Manager, Alexis Levi-Scott, became the first African American female owner in professional basketball when she purchased the team.

Las Vegas Sting Arena Football Team

Bill MacFarland's Nevada Pro Sports was a short-lived effort to build a business around summertime arena sports at the brand-new MGM Grand Garden Arena in Las Vegas in the mid-1990s. While toiling as a minor league hockey player for the Seattle Totems in the 1960s, MacFarland put himself through law school. In the 1970s, MacFarland served as President and Legal Counsel of the World Hockey Association and later took part in a failed effort to secure an NHL expansion franchise for Seattle in the early 1990s. After the Seattle NHL bid failed, MacFarland turned his attention to Las Vegas and the development of MGM Grand Garden.

Nevada Pro Sports' first acquisition was on Dec. 1, 1992. was an expansion franchise in the Continental Indoor Soccer League (CISL). The CISL was a start-up league whose investors included owners and arena operators from the NBA and NHL looking to fill building dates during the slow summer season. With the MGM Grand Garden still under construction in 1993, MacFarland elected to defer the debut of his Las Vegas Dustdevils soccer team until the CISL's sophomore campaign in 1994. Soon afterward, Nevada Pro Sports added an Arena Football League expansion franchise, the Las Vegas Sting, to its portfolio of teams set to debut in the summer of 1994.

Neither team drew much interest in Las Vegas despite an announced crowd of 10,109 into the MGM Grand Garden for their home debut on May 21, 1994, against the Miami Hooters. But by the Sting's third home game in June, attendance plunged below 4,000, and the team finished the year with an average of 6,413, 9th best out of the league's 11 teams.

The Sting assembled the typical Arena Football collection of pro football nomads and castaways. Before joining the Sting, two-year starting quarterback Scooter Molander last played for the Colts -- the Espoo Colts of the Finland Football League. Molander's favorite target in 1994 was Tyrone Thurman. At 5' 3" tall and 135 pounds, the kick return specialist was likely the smallest Division I All-American in college football history back in 1988 at Texas Tech. The Sting's defensive leader was former UNLV standout Carlton Johnson, who earned All-League honors as a Defensive Specialist in 1994.

Las Vegas Storm

The Las Vegas Storm was a junior team in the Western States Hockey League (WSHL). They played at the Las Vegas Ice Center. The team was established as an expansion team for the 2014-2015 campaign and played three seasons. The team suspended operations on Sept. 29, 2017, due to a lack of players. The team worked with the league and other teams to get players spots on other teams in the league.

Las Vegas Strikers

Las Vegas Strikers were an American soccer team founded in 2003. The team was a member of the National Premier Soccer League (NPSL), the fourth tier of the American Soccer Pyramid, and played in the Southwest Conference The Strikers played their home matches at the Bettye Wilson Soccer Complex in Las Vegas. In 2006, the team's management announced that they would spend the 2007 NPSL season on hiatus, but after two seasons on hiatus, the team officially folded in 2008.

Las Vegas Tabagators

Las Vegas Tabagators was an American women's soccer team founded in 2005. The team was a member of the Women's Premier Soccer League, the third tier of women's soccer in the United States and Canada, until 2006, when the team left the league and the franchise was terminated. The team played its home games in the Bettye Wilson Soccer Complex in Las Vegas. The name "Tabagators" came from TAB Contractors, the team's sponsor. Prior to joining the WPSL, the Tabagators were among the most successful youth clubs in the region, having won 5 state titles. The team was associated with the National Premier Soccer League franchise Las Vegas Strikers, which also folded.

Las Vegas Thunder

The Las Vegas Thunder was a professional ice hockey team competing in the International Hockey League. The team's home rink was at the Thomas & Mack Center. They began play in the 1993-1994 season, folding on April 18, 1999. The demise of the franchise was precipitated by the refusal of UNLV officials to negotiate with team owners regarding a new agreement to continue playing at the Thomas & Mack Center after the 1998-1999 season. Without a facility that was suitable even for temporary use, the Thunder had to shut down.

Las Vegas Vipers

The Vegas Vipers were a professional football team based in Vegas. The team was founded by Vince McMahon's Alpha Entertainment as the Tampa Bay Vipers and were an owned-and-operated member of the XFL, owned by RedBird Capital Partners, Dwayne Johnson and Dany Garcia's Alpha Acquico, LLC. The Vipers had a franchise regular season record of 3-12, the worst win percentage among all current XFL teams.

On July 24, 2022, the XFL announced that it would be placing one of its eight teams in the Las Vegas area, and that Rod Woodson would be its head coach. It initially appeared unclear whether this would be an expansion team or a relocation. The Vipers' name would be relocated to Las Vegas in homage to southern Nevada being home to numerous rattlesnakes. The move returned the XFL to a market that previously had a team in the Las Vegas Outlaws.

On August 31, 2023, it was announced that the Vipers would not return to their home stadium, Cashman Field, in 2024. At the time of the original announcement, Las Vegas was the only city in which the XFL had not secured a stadium agreement. By the league's own admission, the process of securing a stadium was "long and tedious," as the Vipers had to negotiate around the other teams using Las Vegas's venues (with Allegiant Stadium, Cashman Field, and Bishop Gorman High School being considered at various points), and the XFL was dead-set against having the Vipers play as a traveling team until a venue could be secured. On Jan. 5, 2023, the day the league's schedule was released, Cashman Field was announced to be the Vipers home stadium for the 2023 season. The move into Cashman Field was done with the full cooperation of the Las Vegas Lights FC, who cooperated with the Vipers in setting out each team's schedule. The league had difficulties getting the playing surface to professional standards and maintaining it; the dried, brown grass had to be painted green (causing the field to become slippery when heavy rains fell during the home opener), divots caused by heavy equipment were noted on the field, ESPN's press box was open-air and covered by a tarp, and the boundary lines painted on the field were found to not be straight. Both the Vipers players and league president Russ Brandon noted that the field was structurally sound and held up well to the harsh conditions.

Las Vegas Wranglers (hockey)

The Las Vegas Wranglers were a professional ice hockey team based in the Las Vegas Valley. The Wranglers were members of the Pacific Division of the Western Conference of the ECHL (formerly the East Coast Hockey League). The Wranglers were founded as an expansion franchise in 2003 following the ECHL's takeover of the West Coast Hockey League.

In May 2014, the team suspended operations for the 2014-15 ECHL season, allowing it time to secure a new home arena. In 2015, the team withdrew from the ECHL after being unable to find a home arena for the 2015-16 season.

The Wranglers won many accolades over their time in the league. They have the highest winning percentage in ECHL history and hold six other ECHL records. The Wranglers made two appearances in the Kelly Cup Finals, in 2008 and 2012 and won the Brabham Cup once and the Pacific Division title twice. Former Wranglers who have reached the National Hockey League (NHL) include Brent Krahn, Adam Pardy, Dany Sabourin, Tyson Strachan and Tyler Sloan. From 2003 to 2014, the Wranglers played their home games at the Orleans Arena. The team's lease with Orleans Arena ended after the 2013-14 season.

The Wranglers had been the ECHL affiliate of the NHL's Calgary Flames since the team's inaugural season in 2003 until 2009 before announcing that they were switching their affiliation to the Phoenix Coyotes for the 2009-10 ECHL season.

The Wranglers garnered many accolades from the local media, including the Las Vegas Review-Journal naming the Wranglers "Best Local Sports Team" three times (2005, 2006, 2009) and head coach Glen Gulutzan "Best Local Coach" (2007, 2009).

Las Vegas Wranglers (baseball)

The Las Vegas Wranglers were a minor league baseball team that played in various leagues in the 1940s and 1950s. They were Las Vegas' first professional team in any sport. he Wranglers were one of the charter franchises of the Class C Sunset League in 1947. Despite Paul Zaby's league-leading .402 batting average and a historic offensive season from Calvin Felix, the Wranglers (a Boston Braves affiliate) finished just 73-67, third place, and were beaten in the semifinals by Riverside, Calif. Las Vegas was managed by ex-major leaguer Newt Kimball, who also won 14 games as a pitcher for the Wranglers that year.

Las Vegas continued to be one of the circuit's top teams for the next three years. In 1948, the Wranglers moved up to second place and made it to the championship series before losing to Reno. However, the team drew only around 600 fans per game (Las Vegas' population was only around 20,000 then) and faced a $15,000 deficit at season's end, partially because they were no longer affiliated with the Braves. In 1949, however, the Wranglers blew the league away with an 88-38 record and easily claimed the pennant, with attendance climbing to over 1,000 per contest. Due to budget cuts, there were no playoffs that year, and the '49 Wranglers had claimed Las Vegas' first pro sports championship (and last one for 37 years, until the Las Vegas Stars won the PCL crown in 1986). After a third-place finish in 1950, the top teams in the Sunset League merged with the Arizona-Mexico League to form the new Southwest International League in 1951.

Declining attendance vexed minor-league ball throughout the country in the early 1950s, and Las Vegas was no exception: despite two more winning seasons in 1951-52, the Wranglers (along with the rest of the SWIL) died after the 1952 season.

Baseball returned to Las Vegas in 1957, but the new team (also called the Wranglers) finished fourth in the Arizona-Mexico League, and then folded. On May 26, 1958, however, the San Jose Pirates of the California League shifted operations to Las Vegas, renaming themselves (once again) the Wranglers. But the team finished a poor seventh and disbanded after the season when the Cal League shrunk from eight teams to six.

Las Vegas would not have another professional baseball team for a quarter-century, until the Las Vegas Stars joined the Pacific Coast League in 1983.

Triple A Baseball

These three teams were never defunct but two of them did change Major League Baseball affiliates until yielding to the Aviators. The Las Vegas Stars minor league baseball team played in the Pacific Coast League from 1983 to 2000. The Stars, playing their games at Cashman Field, were a successful team and were considered the only long-lasting team in city history. They became the Las Vegas 51s of the Los Angeles Dodgers, then the Las Vegas Aviators of the Oakland A's.

The 1983 inaugural Pacific Coast League season was a memorable one in the city of Las Vegas. Triple-A baseball was born on April 10, 1983, before a sellout crowd of 10,622 at Cashman Field. The Stars, in their brown, gold and burnt orange uniforms, defeated Salt Lake City, 11-8. Catcher Bruce Bochy, former San Diego Padres manager and current skipper of the Texas Rangers, hit the first home run in Cashman Field history. The first pitch was delivered by MLB right-hander Andy Hawkins.

Las Vegas, under manager Harry Dunlop, posted a regular season record of 83-60 (.580), the team's best mark that stood for 19 seasons until the 2002 51s broke the all-time record of 85-59 (.590). The Stars were the Triple-A affiliate of the San Diego Padres for 18 seasons (1983-2000).

The team featured outfielder Kevin McReynolds, one of the greatest players in franchise history. He was named the league MVP appeared in 113 games and batted .377 with a team-record 46 doubles, 328 total bases (team record), 32 home runs and 116 RBI. McReynolds enjoyed a 12-year Major League career with San Diego (1983-1986), New York Mets (1987-1991, 1994) and Kansas City (1992-93).

The 1983 Stars helped propel the franchise to many years of success and provided family-oriented entertainment for the citizens of Southern Nevada for 35 seasons.

The Las Vegas Pacific Coast League franchise traces its roots to the Portland Beavers, who entered the PCL in 1919 after a two-year hiatus. The team relocated to Spokane, Wash., in 1973, becoming the Spokane Indians. The franchise moved once again in 1983, becoming the Las Vegas Stars.

The Stars were the first professional sports team to play in Las Vegas since the Las Vegas Wranglers baseball club, who played from 1947 to 1952 and 1957 to 1958. The Stars' inaugural season was quite successful, posting an 83-60 record and winning the first-half championship for the Southern Division, leading to a playoff berth, but eventually losing to the Albuquerque Dukes. The following season, the Stars posted a 71-65 record and won their second division championship (first half), but ultimately lost in the league semifinals to the Hawaii Islanders.

After a dismal 1985 campaign, the Stars finished the 1986 season with an 80-62 record and won the second half of the Southern Division. In the league semifinals, the Stars defeated the Phoenix Firebirds, 3-2, and went on to win their first PCL championship, defeating the Vancouver Canadians in five games. The Stars won their second PCL championship in 1988, once again defeating Vancouver, this time in four games.

After winning five division titles and two league championships in their first six years, the Stars hit a skid, posting a .500 or better record only four times and winning shares of only two division championships in the following 12 years. The Stars were unable to advance past the first round of the playoffs in both seasons that they qualified. The team's affiliation with the Padres ended after the 2000 season. The 1983 Las Vegas Stars team was inducted into the Southern Nevada Sports Hall of Fame on June 8, 2007.

Las Vegas 51s (2001-2018)

The first A Las Vegas 51s baseball game came against the Iowa Cubs at Cashman Field in 2008. In 2001, Las Vegas became the top farm club of the Los Angeles Dodgers. The new affiliation was accompanied by rebranding to the Las Vegas 51s in reference to Area 51, a military base located north-northwest of Las Vegas legendary for rumors of its housing UFOs and extraterrestrial technology. The team adopted a logo featuring a grey alien head and introduced an extraterrestrial mascot named Cosmo.

A new affiliate, moniker and appearance did not translate into improved performance on the field. The 51s experienced only two winning seasons during their eight years as the Triple-A Dodgers. Their only division title came under manager Brad Mills in 2002 when the team posted the best record in the league at 85-59 but lost 3-1 to the eventual PCL Champion Edmonton Trappers.

The Dodgers and the 51s had a rocky relationship during their eight-year affiliation. On March 24, 2008, Mandalay Baseball Properties sold the 51s franchise to Stevens Baseball Group. There were no plans to move the team, and talks of building a new stadium to replace the aging Cashman Field became stagnant.

The Dodgers were not pleased with Cashman Field, which barely met the standards for Triple-A baseball. It had no weight room or indoor batting cages, and it was decrepit compared to other stadiums in the league. Citing the inadequacies of Cashman and lack of planning for a replacement, Los Angeles decided not to renew their player development contract (PDC) with Las Vegas after the 2008 season.

Following the departure of the Los Angeles Dodgers, the 51s signed with the Toronto Blue Jays, marking the first time that the 51s were affiliated with an American League club. The only time the team finished over .500 with the Blue Jays was in 2012 when Marty Brown led the team to a 79-64 second-place finish. The Blue Jays ended their affiliation with the 51s after the season.

In April 2013, the team was purchased by Summerlin Las Vegas Baseball Club LLC, a joint venture of Howard Hughes Corp and Play Ball Owners Group, including investors Steve Mack, Bart Wear, and Chris Kaempfer, with intentions of moving it to a proposed stadium in Summerlin near the Red Rock Resort Spa and Casino. The 51s became affiliated with the New York Mets in 2013 when they were the only Triple-A team left without an MLB parent. They won back-to-back division titles in 2013 and 2014 under manager Wally Backman but were eliminated in the Pacific Conference championship series on both occasions.

In 2017, the 51s became one of the first teams to participate in the Copa de la Diversión initiative and for selected games played as the Reyes de Plata ("Silver Kings"). The name was a nod to Nevada being the "Silver State" and a homage to the contribution migrant workers made to the mining industry of Nevada. In October 2017, the Las Vegas Convention and Visitors Authority approved a 20-year, $80 million naming rights agreement to help pay for the new $150 million 10,000-seat ballpark, which opened in 2019. Las Vegas Ballpark, located in Summerlin, includes 22 suites, a center field pool, a kids' zone and numerous bars.Construction began in 2018 and was completed for the 2019 season. In late 2017, the Mets announced plans to move its affiliation to the Syracuse Mets beginning in 2019, meaning the 51s would be in need of a new major league affiliate.

Las Vegas Aviators (2019-present)

The Las Vegas Aviators, formerly known as the Las Vegas 51s and Las Vegas Stars, are a Minor League Baseball team of the Pacific Coast League (PCL) and the Triple-A affiliate of the Oakland Athletics. Now that the Oakland franchise is preparing to move to Las Vegas, t he future of the Aviators is in doubt.They are located in Summerlin South. The team has been members of the Pacific Coast League since 1983, including the 2021 season when it was known as the Triple-A West, and won the PCL championship as the Stars in 1986 and 1988.

Following the conclusion of the 2018 season, Las Vegas signed a two-year contract with the Oakland Athletics. In addition to having a new major league affiliate in 2019 and playing in a new ballpark, the team also changed its name to the Las Vegas Aviators. The name is in reference to aviation pioneer Howard Hughes. The team's new logo depicts a pilot wearing a helmet. Their first home game at Las Vegas Ballpark was before a sellout crowd of 11,036.

Chapter 13
The Kingdom of the Golden Knights Is Forged

The Vegas Golden Knights' journey from expansion franchise to Stanley Cup Champions resulted from strategic player acquisitions, effective coaching, strong team chemistry, and astute salary cap management. Their rapid rise to success is a testament to the organization's ability to build a winning team quickly.

"People from Las Vegas wanted something more than the Strip. They wanted something that was theirs. So, we tapped into that," Owner Bill Foley said after winning the Cup.

Even though the team came close in year one – placing second to the Washington Capitals – to win in season six meant having the pieces in place, one by one. The solid foundation laid during the expansion draft, followed by a commitment to building a dominant team through trades, came about finding the right coach to lead them. Here's how the construction of the Cup team occurred.

The History

After Jerry Bruckheimer halted his attempt to lure a team to Las Vegas, rumors of a Las Vegas expansion team surfaced again in August of 2014, pointing to a new indoor arena on the Strip (built as a joint venture between Anschutz Entertainment Group, owners of the Los Angeles Kings, and MGM Resorts International) as the potential home arena, although these rumors were denied by the league. In November 2014, an unconfirmed report stated that the league had selected billionaire businessman Foley and the Maloof family (former owners of the National Basketball Association's Sacramento Kings, and founders of the Palms Casino Resort) to lead the ownership group of Black Knight Sports and Entertainment for a possible Las Vegas expansion team. In Dec. 2014, the NHL's board of governors decided to allow Foley to hold a season ticket drive to gauge interest in a Las Vegas team, though league commissioner Gary Bettman also asked the media not to "make more out of this than it is."

The season ticket drive began in February 2015 with interested parties placing ten percent deposits for the 2016-2017 season. The drive drew 5,000 deposits in its first day and a half and reached its goal of 10,000 deposits by April 2015. In June 2015, the league officially opened the window for prospective owners to bid on expansion teams.

By this point, Foley had secured more than 13,200 season ticket deposits. Two expansion applications were submitted: Foley's application for a Las Vegas team, and a bid from Quebecor to revive the Quebec Nordiques at a new arena in Quebec City. Both Las Vegas and Quebec were invited to move into Phase II of the league expansion bid in August 2015, which involved providing additional details about the Las Vegas market to the league. Later in the same month, both bids proceeded to Phase III, which involved a review of ownership financials.

At the league owners' meeting on June 22, 2016, in Las Vegas, the Las Vegas expansion bid was approved by a unanimous vote, with play to begin in the 2017-2018 NHL season. The team became the first major professional sports franchise to be based in Las Vegas, and the first NHL expansion team since 2000. Foley committed to pay the league's $500 million expansion fee and began the process of hiring the team's principal staff and determining its official identity. The team's first office was located next to a porn studio.

Foley announced that former Washington Capitals General Manager George McPhee would be the franchise's first general manager. On Nov. 22, 2016, the name was revealed as the Vegas Golden Knights.

Their home games were set to be played at the newly built T-Mobile Arena on the Las Vegas Strip, nicknamed The Fortress. Bill Foley's leadership and the work of the management team played significant roles in their success. The Golden Knights' bold and strategic approach to roster building, along with Foley's financial expertise, played a significant role in their journey to becoming a successful NHL franchise.

On Feb. 1, 2018, the Golden Knights set the expansion team record for wins in a debut season with 34 wins after only 50 games, and on Feb. 21, 2018, set a record for most points by an expansion team in an inaugural season with 84. Clinching a berth for the 2018 playoffs on March 26, the Golden Knights became the first team since the Edmonton Oilers and Hartford Whalers in the 1979-1980 season to make the playoffs in their inaugural season in the league. On March 31, the Golden Knights clinched the Pacific Division title, becoming the first true expansion team in the four major sports to win its division in its inaugural season (not counting all-expansion divisions, as was the case in the 1967-1968 season). Vegas' inaugural season was widely considered the most successful of any North American expansion team, with much attention given to the breakout seasons of their expansion draft selections, dubbed the "Golden Misfits."

Foley's Golden Touch

Foley's background as an investor began during his time at West Point. He studied technical analysis and closely followed financial markets, tracking around 30 stocks, particularly in growth industries like regional airlines. His dedication to understanding the market and a strong interest in technical analysis led to significant profits.

Foley was a self-taught investor while attending West Point. He devoured books about technical analysis. He read The Wall Street Journal each day to track around 30 stocks on his self-created charts in growth industries – such as regional airlines, with their consolidation in the market making Foley a considerable profit.

Foley's classmates initially doubted his investment skills and expected him to lose his money. However, he defied those expectations through his strategic approach to investing. His classmates expected he'd lose all his money. He didn't ... at least not until Foley blew the money on "women and alcohol," by his own admission.

Later in life, after a law degree and an MBA, he made enough money to pool it with other investors to buy what would become Fidelity National Financial, the biggest insurance title company in the U.S., as well as other businesses. His investment philosophy will sound familiar to anyone who has followed the Knights: a "value buyer" who made around 80 acquisitions that Foley estimated were valued at $40 million that they paid $20 million to get.

He applied his investment knowledge to the world of hockey. Foley's journey as a self-taught investor and the strategic decisions made by the Las Vegas Golden Knights in building their roster were fascinating aspects of the team's history.

Foley's ultimate goal for the team was not just winning a Stanley Cup but establishing a dynasty by winning multiple Stanley Cups over several years.

"My goal is to be a dynasty here," Foley said. "Not to win a Stanley Cup. Multiple Stanley Cups over several years."

His bold statements included worldwide appeal.

"We want to be a global franchise," Foley said early on. "Visitors to Las Vegas can't get a ticket because we're sold out, but they're going to buy gear. They're going to be back in Shanghai wearing a Golden Knights hat."

Coming Up a Winner

Foley played the largest role in selecting the team's leadership, including general manager George McPhee and assistant general manager Kelly McCrimmon. McPhee's legal background and McCrimmon's business acumen complemented each other. McPhee had a law degree. McCrimmon had a business degree.

McPhee and his team played key roles in player scouting and salary cap management.

"It was about putting the right people in place in our hockey operations department. We were prepared, I can tell you that. That's the secret to our success," Foley said.

"I really think the NHL erred in how they treated the expansion teams, all the way up until Vegas," former Nashville general manager David Poile told The Associated Press. "We made [the previous teams'] trek much more difficult than it needed to be."

Ahead of that draft, Foley had interviewed several potential general managers, but he instantly felt McPhee, who had led the Washington Capitals for nearly 20 years, was his guy.

"He wanted to win and didn't want anything to stand in his way of the Stanley Cup, period," Foley said.

Wayne Gretzky believes George McPhee's presence as the team's general manager was critical.

"I think George McPhee is one of the hardest working people that we've ever had in the game," Gretzky said. "He's had the experiences of being in Vancouver, places like the New York Islanders and Washington. "I think this franchise is going to be very strong, and it's going to do very well."

2017 Expansion Draft

Perhaps the single most influential event that led to the immediate success was the Expansion Draft, where they had considerable success in selecting players. After Foley paid $500 million for entry, the NHL changed its expansion draft rules to make Vegas competitive off the jump.

The foundation of the Golden Knights' roster was set when the Expansion Draft Rules did not force teams to pay their dues with marginal talent. The Knights could draft the eighth-best forward, fourth-

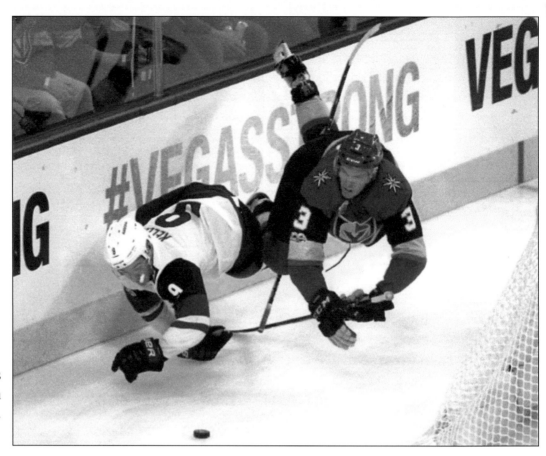

Brayden McNAbb is an original Golden Knight Misfit.

best defenseman or second-best goalie from each team.

"First of all, we're so much smarter now, in all aspects in life," Gretzky told the NHL Network in 2017. "In 1967 (the league's first expansion), when we started with the six teams…you get the worst players you could possibly have. And they were bad for years and years, and people said, 'Well, that's not a hockey city, and you can't survive there.' So the Commissioner (Gary Bettman), and their office and the (Players') Union are smart enough to get together now and say: 'Listen, we've got to put a half decent product there.' So, people say: 'You know what, I love watching the team compete. They play hard, we know they're a young team, we know they're going to get better, and we've got a chance.' Instead of putting the worst team you can put together and then saying after two years, you know what, Las Vegas is not a hockey city. And that's not fair to the city, and that's not fair to the National Hockey League.

"So, I think they're going to be very successful," Gretzky predicted.

McPhee and McCrimmon split the league in half for the draft. The new rules meant that teams would have to leave players they didn't want to lose unprotected in the draft. The rules changes afforded the Knights two hefty advantages: the leverage of the draft rules and a clean salary cap. Teams had to leave key, high-salaried players unprotected, so the Golden Knights held a

distinct advantage. They leveraged the draft rules and their clean salary cap to assemble a competitive team.

He had the opportunity to form his own financial landscape.

"We were around the fringes," Foley said of the team's salary cap management:

The team's ability to manage the salary cap effectively was crucial to their success due to other teams dealing with cap constraints. However, they eventually faced financial challenges and had to make difficult decisions as they reached the salary cap limit.

"They were ruthless and prepared," one NHL source recalled.

Larry Brooks of the New York Post recently argued that the "greatest weapon" the Golden Knights and the Seattle Kraken were awarded upon entry into the NHL was not the liberal expansion rules but rather their pristine salary cap space.

"If right now teams could renounce their rosters in exchange for $83.5M in cap space entering this off-season, how many do you think would stand pat with current personnel and how many would opt to begin again?" Brooks wrote.

"I really think the NHL erred in how they treated the expansion teams, all the way up until Vegas," former Nashville general manager David Poile told The Associated Press. "We made the previous teams' trek much more difficult than it needed to be."

Six members of the 2023 Stanley Cup team were selected throughout the 2017 Expansion Draft, including:

• Jonathan Marchessault was the Knight's best selection. In a surprising move, the Florida Panthers traded Reilly Smith to Vegas, which allowed the Golden Knights to select Jonathan Marchessault. The Panthers aimed to keep defensemen Mark Pysyk and Alex Petrovic. Marchessault and Smith became integral parts of the Golden Knights' success, highlighting the unpredictability of NHL decisions. He was a star winger and played an instrumental role in the team's success. Ironically, he went on to win the Conn Smythe Trophy as the playoff MVP in 2023. His offensive prowess and leadership on the ice were invaluable to the Golden Knights. "You know what? I thought they were going to protect me," Marchessault told ESPN this past postseason. "I was surprised of the decision. But I mean, that's just the way she goes sometimes. Keeps you honest."

• William Karlsson was acquired via a draft night trade. On 21 June 2017, having been left "exposed" by Columbus for the 2017 NHL Expansion Draft, Karlsson was selected by the Vegas Golden Knights. The Blue Jackets traded a first-round pick, a second-round pick in 2019 and injured forward David Clarkson to Vegas with the agreement that the Golden Knights would select Karlsson. He emerged as a key offensive force for the Golden Knights, known for his goal-scoring ability. Karlsson's production as a top-line center was a significant factor in the team's early success. He was drafted in the second round, 53rd overall, by the Anaheim Ducks in the 2011 NHL Entry Draft. In addition to playing for Vegas, Karlsson has also played in the NHL for Anaheim and the Columbus Blue Jackets. The Blue Jackets traded their 2017 first-round pick and center William Karlsson to the Knights so they'd take David Clarkson's contract instead of either forward Josh Anderson or goaltender Joonas Korpisalo.

• Shea Theodore was acquired from the Anaheim Ducks via the draft night trade. The Anaheim Ducks exposed several quality defensemen, including Josh Manson and Sami Vatanen. To ensure Vegas selected defenseman Clayton Stoner, the Ducks traded promising 21-year-old defenseman Theodore to the Golden Knights. Theodore became a crucial player for Vegas, ranking second in average ice time during their Stanley Cup run. He developed into a top-tier defenseman, providing offensive production from the blue line. His contributions, including a goal and five assists in the Stanley Cup Final, highlighted his importance to the team.

• Reilly Smith was acquired from the Florida Pan-

thers via draft night trade, further strengthening Vegas' forward depth. He was a consistent offensive contributor and played a complementary role alongside other top forwards. The Florida Panthers, in one of the most mind-boggling moves in NHL history, traded forward Smith to the Knights so Vegas would select 30-goal scorer Marchessault in the draft; in turn, the Panthers could keep defensemen Pysyk and Petrovic. Florid GM Dale Tallon said at the time that "you win championships with defense." Instead, the Knights won with Marchessault and Smith.

• William Carrier added depth to the team's forward lines and provided a physical presence on the ice. While not always reflected on the scoresheet, his contributions were appreciated by the coaching staff and teammates. The Buffalo Sabres traded a sixth-round pick to Vegas so they'd select Carrier in the draft instead of goalie prospect Linus Ullmark. Carrier was the key component of the Knights' bruising checking line this postseason.

• Brayden McNabb, a defenseman, brought a physical and defensive element to the team's blue line. His two assists in the Stanley Cup Final demonstrated his ability to contribute offensively when needed. The Los Angeles Kings dangled veteran forwards Dustin Brown and Marian Gaborik in front of McPhee. Instead, he selected 26-year-old McNabb, who appeared in all but one playoff game in 2023.

The Knights knew they had won the draft. Even if they ended up trading these players they had gathered, they had done well.

Sometimes, it was moves that led to future moves, like when the Minnesota Wild sent top prospect Alex Tuch to the Knights so they'd select forward Erik Haula instead of players such as Matt Dumba or Marco Scandella. Tuch would be a key component of the Jack Eichel trade in 2021. Other times, it was using cap space to acquire substantial talent immediately, like when Marc-Andre Fleury was selected from the Pittsburgh Penguins.

After the Expansion Draft, the Las Vegas sportsbooks had Vegas at 250-1 to win the Stanley Cup – the worst odds in the league. The actual Newsweek headline on the expansion draft: One prognosticator predicted, "The Vegas Golden Knights Are Going To Suck in 2017-18." What neither the team nor its critics realized: The foundation for this championship team had been laid by McPhee and McCrimmon in that expansion draft.

Movers and Shakers

Over the years, the Golden Knights made strategic

moves to bolster their roster. In 2019, they acquired star winger Mark Stone, and in November 2021, they pulled off a blockbuster trade for star center Jack Eichel. Eichel became available in the trade market because the Sabres wouldn't let Eichel get the artificial disk herniation surgery he desired. The ugly power struggle between Eichel – who had previously requested a trade – and the team led to him being traded. Calgary and other teams were in the mix. Vegas wasn't about to allow him to slip away, and it was willing to have him get the surgery.

Eichel's acquisition gave the Golden Knights a bona fide No. 1 center, addressing a crucial need in their lineup. Eichel's competitiveness and leadership qualities have been evident, and he has thrived in the team's supportive environment.

Again, the Knights collected someone who was not

wanted. The Sabres weren't going to allow Eichel to have the artificial disk replacement surgery he believed was the only way to repair his injured neck. But no NHL player had ever had the procedure.

After getting his preferred surgery, Eichel made his return to the ice on Feb. 16, 2022. Eichel tallied 14 goals and 11 assists in 34 games in his first stretch back on the ice. While Eichel's first season back was a success, the Golden Knights dealt with injuries to multiple players throughout the year and missed the postseason for the first time in franchise history.

"It means the world here. I mean, can't say enough good things about this whole organization," Eichel said. "Obviously, everything that they did to allow me to get back to playing, but just even the way that they take care of you. It really feels like a big family, and everyone cares for each other and they really look out for you. The people at the top do so much for this organization. And it just trickles down. And we feel the love in here as a team, and I feel really proud to be a part of this organization."

Prior to the 2018-2019 season, the Golden Knights acquired winger Max Pacioretty from the Montreal Canadiens and signed free-agent center Paul Stastny, filling the roster holes left by the free-agency departures of James Neal and David Perron. Additionally, Vegas acquired future captain Stone from the Ottawa Senators at the trade deadline, subsequently signing him to an eight-year extension. Stone quickly became a cornerstone player for the franchise, signing an eight-year, $76 million contract extension. During the 2018-2019 season and the playoffs, Stone showcased his offensive prowess, recording 12 points (six goals and six assists) in the playoffs. However, injuries limited his regular-season appearances in subsequent years.

Despite dropping to 93 standings points from the prior season's 109, the Golden Knights returned to the playoffs as the third seed in the Pacific Division. They ultimately suffered their first-ever first-round elimination, losing to the San Jose Sharks in seven games after leading the series 3 games to 1. Game seven was particularly notable; after taking a 3-0 lead into the third period, Cody Eakin delivered a cross-check to Sharks captain Joe Pavelski, resulting in a controversial 5-minute major penalty call that saw the Sharks score four goals and take a 4–3 lead. The Sharks would eventually win the game despite a late game-tying goal by Marchessault for Vegas that was followed by Barclay Goodrow's series winner in overtime.

In May 2019, Vegas modified their front-office staff, with the promotions of McPhee from general manager to president of hockey operations and assistant general manager McCrimmon to general manager. During the remainder of the off-season and 2019-2020 season, the Golden Knights' roster experienced considerable turnover. In June, original Golden Knights Erik Haula and Colin Miller were traded to the Carolina Hurricanes and Buffalo Sabres, respectively, with recently signed KHL standout Nikita Gusev also being sent to the New Jersey Devils. The team additionally acquired center Chandler Stephenson from the Washington Capitals in early December 2019. After an up-and-down start resulting in a 24-19-6 record and capped by a four-game losing streak, the team fired head coach Gerard Gallant, replacing him with recently fired former Sharks head coach Peter DeBoer on Jan.15, 2020.

But as one family arrives, another one leaves. Foley was concerned team chemistry might suffer without Schmidt. But McPhee and McCrimmon sold Foley on Alex Pietrangelo and on the necessity to move Schmidt's contract off the cap to make room for him.

During the following month, in the lead-up to the trade deadline, Vegas acquired defenseman Alec Martinez from the Los Angeles Kings, forward Nick Cousins from Montreal, and goaltender Robin Lehner from the Chicago Blackhawks, as well as trading original Golden Knights Cody Eakin to the Winnipeg Jets and Malcolm Subban to Chicago. Due to the COVID-19 pandemic, the NHL regular season was suspended on March 12, 2020, and officially concluded on May 26. Vegas, holding the best points percentage in the Western Conference, automatically qualified for the re-structured playoffs, playing in a round-robin to determine the top four seeds in the Western playoff bracket. After sweeping the round-robin rounds over the Dallas Stars, St. Louis Blues, and Colorado Avalanche, Vegas earned the first seed, defeating Chicago in the first round in five games. In the second round, Vegas defeated the Vancouver Canucks in seven games.

Their playoff run would end in the Western Conference Finals, however, as the Knights lost to Dallas in five games.

Prior to the shortened 2020-2021 season, Stone was named the first captain in franchise history. Additionally, alternate captain and team leader Deryk Engelland retired, stepping into a front-office role with the team. The Golden Knights further overhauled the roster in the off-season, notably signing defenseman Alex Pietrangelo to a seven-year contract, as well as trading Paul Stastny to Winnipeg and original Golden Knight Nate Schmidt to Vancouver.

"It was a tough pill to swallow," a distraught Schmidt said at the time.

The shortened schedule saw a temporary realignment where teams only played against their own division in the regular season, with Vegas being placed in a new eight-team West Division. The Golden Knights ultimately finished second in both the division and league, despite being tied in points with the Colorado Avalanche. The Avalanche had five more regulation wins than Vegas.

In the first round of the playoffs, Vegas was forced to a game seven for the third consecutive year after leading 3-1 but defeated the Minnesota Wild thanks in part to a hat trick from trade-deadline acquisition Mattias Janmark. In the second round, the Golden Knights defeated the Avalanche in six games despite initially going down 2-0. Vegas' playoff run would again end one round short of the Stanley Cup Finals as the Golden Knights were then upset by the Montreal

Canadiens in six games in the Stanley Cup semifinals. Goaltender Marc-Andre Fleury was named the winner of the Vezina Trophy as the league's best goaltender at season's end, with he and Lehner also sharing the William M. Jennings Trophy win for allowing the fewest goals against of any team.

The 2021 off-season began with a swap of former first-round picks, as Vegas acquired Nolan Patrick from the Philadelphia Flyers as part of a three-team trade that sent Cody Glass to the Nashville Predators. Vegas also acquired forward Brett Howden from the New York Rangers, later sending Ryan Reaves to the Rangers in a separate trade. Most controversially, Fleury was traded to Chicago for minor-league forward Mikael Hakkarainen due to salary-cap constraints. Vegas later traded for Ottawa Senators forward Evgenii Dadonov, as well as signing Laurent Brossoit to back up Lehner.

Approximately one month after the start of the 2021-2022 season, Vegas acquired Eichel from the Buffalo Sabres in exchange for Tuch, Peyton Krebs, and two draft picks. During the course of the season, the Golden Knights suffered a rash of injuries across the roster, with a total of 478 man-games lost; owing to this, Ben Hutton, Michael Amadio, Adam Brooks, and Derrick Pouliot were signed or claimed off waivers for depth, while rookies such as Jake Leschyshyn, Jonas Rondbjerg, and Logan Thompson received significant playing time.

The trade deadline also witnessed a voided trade, as an attempt to send Dadonov to the Anaheim Ducks fell through due to non-compliance with his no-trade clause. Due in part to the injuries, as well as lackluster play, the Golden Knights ultimately missed the playoffs for the first time in team history, finishing three points behind the Nashville Predators in the Western Conference.

The acquisition of Eichel in November 2021 exemplified the team's strategy of collecting talented players who may be undervalued or unwanted by their previous teams. Eichel's surgery preferences added an extra layer of complexity to the trade. The team's ability to acquire players like Eichel and navigate the salary cap demonstrated their strategic approach to building a competitive roster. Many transactions contributed.

Max Pacioretty was acquired by the Golden Knights in 2018 as a key part of the team's offense. However, in the 2022 offseason, the team traded Pacioretty to the Carolina Hurricanes to further address their salary cap concerns. This move required the Golden Knights to rely on other players, like Brett Howden and Nicolas Roy, to fill the offensive void left by Pacioretty.

While Pacioretty was a significant contributor during his time in Vegas, the trade allowed the team to reallocate cap space and potentially make other moves to improve the roster.

Toughest Cap Decision

The Knights weren't immune from financial mistakes. Much of the pain caused by the departure of beloved players was directly related to the team being capped out. But they also maneuvered their way around the problems.

After the salary cap was maxed out, the team faced challenges related to the salary cap and a few overreaching financial mistakes, which led to the departure of beloved players. The pursuit of a championship often requires tough decisions, and the Golden Knights made significant roster changes in recent years. Players like Schmidt, Fleury, Stastny, Pacioretty, and coach Gerard Gallant, who were essential to the team at one point, saw changes in their roles.

Marc-Andre Fleury had an outstanding 2020-21 season, winning the Vezina Trophy as the league's top goaltender with a remarkable 1.98 goals-against-average.

Despite his excellent performance, the Golden Knights faced salary cap challenges that necessitated tough decisions. Fleury was traded to the Chicago Blackhawks, marking the first time a Vezina Trophy winner had been traded since Dominik Hasek in 2001. This move allowed the Golden Knights to free up valuable salary cap space, which could be used to address other roster needs and maintain financial flexibility.

While it was undoubtedly a difficult decision, it demonstrated the team's commitment to making the necessary moves to remain competitive while managing their cap situation.

Appearing on "The Cam & Strick Podcast" in 2021, Foley sought to quiet speculation about Fleury's future with the team amid rather loud trade rumors. He told a story about Foley being in an elevator with Fleury and his wife during the inaugural season.

Foley said: "I told him, 'You're going to retire here.' He said, 'What do you mean?' I said, 'This is where you're going to be. You're going to love Vegas. Vegas is going to love you.' I feel like I made a commitment to him at that point."

Five months after that podcast aired, Fleury was traded to the Chicago Blackhawks. Many still feel the Knights did Fleury wrong. He was the face of the franchise, and the team's first true star, leading them to the Stanley Cup Final in their inaugural season and winning the Vezina Trophy in 2020-21.

The story of Fleury's slow divorce with the Knights is hockey lore now, including when his agent, Allan Walsh, infamously tweeted an image of the goalie with a sword in his back – adorned with the name of then-Vegas coach Pete DeBoer.

But the turnover of the roster has been a hallmark of the franchise.

"It happened right after that first year, right? Those were some of the biggest changes," McNabb said. "You kind of just understand the business. You get close to guys, become close friends. The longer you play in this league, the more you know that it's just the way it is."

But at what cost? It's not that the Knights made these moves. Every team does. It's how they made them that's the problem for some.

"What kind of carnage is left in their wake?" one NHL source asked.

These decisions reflect the challenging nature of managing an NHL team's salary cap while striving for success. The Golden Knights' willingness to make tough choices demonstrated their commitment to building a competitive team within the constraints of the salary cap system. Ultimately, their roster adjustments and other acquisitions, such as Eichel, paid off as they secured the Stanley Cup in the 2023 season.

Franchise Extras

On May 16, 2017, the Golden Knights entered a multi-year affiliation agreement with a minor league team, the Chicago Wolves of the American Hockey League. Like most NHL-AHL affiliation arrangements, the Golden Knights were able to transfer players to and from the Wolves. Although the Wolves were the Golden Knights affiliate, the two teams do not share the same ownership.

Logo and Apparel

The team's primary logo is a barbute helmet superimposed on a black and gold shield with a V-shaped opening. The secondary logo is two crossing swords behind a red star, designed to resemble the star found on the landmark Welcome to Fabulous Las Vegas sign. The team's primary color is steel gray, which is said to represent "strength and durability." The other team colors are gold, red (found in the Las Vegas skyline and at Red Rock Canyon), and black (for power and intensity).

The first uniforms in Golden Knights team history were unveiled publicly on June 20, 2017. Home uniforms were steel gray with black, gold and red stripes, while road uniforms were white with steel gray, gold and red stripes. Shoulders featured the alternate swords logo). On Oct.2, 2020, the Golden Knights introduced a gold alternate uniform, essentially a palette swap of the road uniforms with gold and white switching places. On Feb. 11, 2021, the Golden Knights debuted shiny gold helmets as an alternate to their home gray helmets. Starting with the 2022-23 season, the gold uniforms became the primary, while the gray uniforms became the alternate.

The Golden Knights also released a special "Reverse Retro" alternate uniform. Because the Golden Knights did not have a long NHL history to draw from, their retro design was inspired in part by Manon Rhéaume, the first female NHL player who played for the now-defunct Thunder. The uniform employs a red base and features the "crossing swords" logo in front. Their second "Reverse Retro" uniform was a faux-back design, featuring a black base and a diagonal "VEGAS" wordmark inspired by various vintage hotels in the strip. The wordmark also has a glow-in-the-dark feature when shown on a dark background.

The team's name includes "Knights" as a homage to the Black Knights of the United States Military Academy, Foley's alma mater, and because knights were, according to Foley, "the epitome of the warrior class." Foley had hoped to name his team the Black Knights but dropped that plan after encountering resistance from federal officials. Foley was unable to call the team the "Vegas Knights" because the London Knights owned the "Knights" name in Canada.

"Golden" was included in the name because gold is, as Foley stated, the "No. 1 precious metal" and because Nevada is the largest gold-producing state in the country. "Las" was omitted from the team's name because, according to Foley, residents tend to refer to the city simply as "Vegas" and because a four-word name would have been too long.

The United States Army opposed the team's trademark registration because their exhibition parachute team uses the same nickname; they dropped their opposition after negotiating a trademark coexistence agreement with the team.

An objection was also raised by the College of Saint Rose because its sports teams use the same name. The Vegas team's initial trademark application was denied as a result but was later approved on appeal. The team did clear the name with Clarkson University, which also uses the name Golden Knights.

Chapter 14
Golden Knights Hoist the Cup

The Golden Knights' 2022-2023 Stanley Cup-winning season was marked by key events that ultimately led them to the top of the NHL. Their quest was fueled by the team's ability to adapt to changes, make strategic moves, and ultimately win the most coveted prize in hockey. Under the leadership of Coach Bruce Cassidy and with the contributions of key players like Jonathan Marchessault, Jack Eichel, Mark Stone and Adin Hill, Las Vegas received its first major sports title.

The Golden Knights' ability to navigate the salary cap system, make strategic trades and maintain a cohesive team culture have been instrumental in their journey to becoming champions. Their success serves as an example of effective roster management within the constraints of the NHL's financial regulations. These decisions coincided with the challenging nature of managing an NHL team's salary cap while striving for success. Ultimately, their roster adjustments and other acquisitions, such as Eichel and Hill, paid off as they secured Lord Stanley's Cup in the 2023 season, their sixth in the league. The road was rocky as the Knights didn't clinch their division until the final game of the regular season.

Out of Nowhere

Jonathan Marchessault received the Conn Smythe Trophy as the most valuable player during the play-offs, and deservedly so. His spectacular two-way play and timely goal scoring made him a bona fide super-star. But perhaps the most important ingredient to winning any Stanley Cup is to have a hot goaltender. The Knights used five goaltenders during the season before turning to Adin Hill eight games into the Cup conquest.

Sean Burke, the Knights' director of goaltending, knew Hill from their days together with the Arizona Coyotes. His contract was cheap. He was available, thanks to a crowded crease in San Jose. The Knights thought maybe he could help. Instead, Hill's strong performance as the starter is now legendary.

"If you ask any player in the NHL who's ever won a Cup, I guarantee you, besides having kids and getting married, it's one of the top moments of their life," Hill said. "In my career, as a child growing up, you face adversity. You get cut from teams or don't make the team you wanted to. Everybody's got bumps in the road. It's just a matter of sticking to the plan and not changing your course of action."

Now he's a Stanley Cup Champion.

The Knights pivoting to Hill was transformative for the team. He played the best hockey of his career, and his exceptional performance helped elevate the Golden Knights' all-around play. Hill's performance in the 2023 postseason was nothing short of remarkable. He compiled an 11-4-0 record with a 2.17 goals-against-average and an impressive .932 save percentage. Hill's standout performance was particularly evident during the Stanley Cup Finals.

The Golden Knights faced critical goaltending decisions in the 2022-23 season and during the Stanley Cup run. The team faced an early setback when starting goaltender Robin Lehner had to undergo hip surgery, causing him to miss the entire season. Laurent Brossoit was initially chosen as the starting goaltender for the first eight playoff games, but his performance, with a goals-against-average of 3.18, didn't meet expectations. This prompted Cassidy to make a change and turn to Hill.

As an unrestricted free agent after the season, Hill's future with the team became a topic of interest and speculation until he signed a new deal for $5 million a year, a hefty but well-deserved salary for a NHL playoff goalie.

Here's a summary of other formidable Cup-winning ingredients:

The hiring of Cassidy: After a disappointing season that saw the team miss the playoffs for the first time in franchise history under Peter DeBoer, Cassidy was brought in as the head coach. Cassidy, known for his success with the Boston Bruins, took over the reins and quickly established a better locker room atmosphere after falling short of winning the Stanley Cup with the Bruins in 2019. Cassidy's emphasis on defense, his ability to get the players to buy into his system, and his overall coaching acumen played a crucial role in the Golden Knights' journey. His impact was particularly evident in the team's improved defensive play and the development of key players such as Eichel. Cassidy's hiring marked a turning point for the franchise and helped them reach the pinnacle of success in just his first season as the leader.

Eichel's Facilitating Ability: Jack Eichel's role as a facilitator was crucial to the Golden Knights' success.

Jonathan Marchessault skates with the Stanley Cup after trouncing Florida.

His ability to set up plays with skilled puck handling was monumental. Following an ugly power struggle between Eichel and the Buffalo Sabres, the All-Star Center requested to be traded to another NHL team. The Calgary Flames were among the teams that wanted him. But Las Vegas wasn't about to allow Eichel to slip away, and management was willing to have him get the surgery he wanted instead of what Buffalo desired.

"It means the world here. I mean, can't say enough good things about this whole organization," Eichel said. "Obviously, everything that they did to allow me to get back to playing, but just even the way that they take care of you. It really feels like a big family, and everyone cares for each other, and they really look out for you."

While the Golden Knights missed the playoffs during Eichel's first partial season due to various injuries to key players, the 2022-23 season saw a resurgence. Eichel compiled 66 points during the regular season, showcasing his scoring and playmaking abilities. Eichel also elevated his game in the playoffs, leading the team with 25 points (six goals and 20 assists). His dynamic two-way play was instrumental in the team's championship run.

Of course, any discussion of Eichel, who earns $10 million annually, instigates a discussion of the Golden Knights' salary cap gymnastics. Vegas has navigated the system since it added its first player in 2017, and it worked the rules to win a Stanley Cup.

Dominating forward Stone earns $9.5 million annually, a salary that was buried on long-term injured reserve from February through the start of the playoffs, which enabled the Golden Knights to add more salary at the trade deadline. Stone's return for the 2023 playoffs was pivotal. He contributed 24 points (11 goals and 13 assists) during the postseason, including a memorable hat trick in Game 5 of the Stanley Cup Final. Even amidst injury challenges, Stone's leadership and clutch performances were integral to the Golden Knights' triumph.

Stone was activated from injured reserve in time for Game 1 of their first-round series against the Winnipeg Jets on April 18 – five days after he missed the finale of their regular season, the last game in which they had to worry about being cap-compliant.

"He had back surgery, and there was just as likely a chance his career was at risk as there was no assurance he'd be back for the playoffs," GM Kelly McCrimmon told the Las Vegas Review-Journal in April. Anything to suggest this was orchestrated and timed out is inaccurate and disrespectful to Mark and the organization."

Defense: The Knights had no one in the top 60 in scoring in the league but had Alec Martinex (244) first and Brayden McNabb second (198) in blocked shots with Alex Petrangelo seventh with 177.

Trades: The Golden Knights' rise is rooted in their ability to make strategic moves aside from the Eichel deal. For instance, acquiring players like Alex Tuch through previous deals, who later became integral in the Eichel trade, demonstrated the team's foresight in building their roster.

In an effort to clear salary cap space, the Golden Knights traded star forward Max Pacioretty to the Carolina Hurricanes. This move necessitated relying on role players like Brett Howden and Nicolas Roy to fill the gap left by Pacioretty. Pacioretty was acquired by the Golden Knights in 2018 and was a key part of the team's offense. The trade also allowed the team to reallocate cap space and potentially make other moves to improve the roster. The Knights also picked up veteran winger Ivan Barbashev at the trade deadline. His hustle and hitting in the Finals often went unnoticed by some. His work around the boards is extraordinary.

McCrimmon, who had been elevated to Vegas general manager in 2019 while George McPhee stepped up to a team president role, said he and the Knights management decided that landing a top-pairing defenseman was a priority while watching them fall short in the bubble.

"When you looked at the teams that were winning, we felt we needed a No. 1 defenseman. Like a Victor Hedman. Like an Alex Pietrangelo," he said. "To be a Stanley Cup-contending team, we had to be better there. So, we were aggressive in free agency."

As it turns out, the actual Alex Pietrangelo was available as he couldn't come to contract terms with the St. Louis Blues. He was open to Vegas as an option, and the team aggressively courted him.

"It's always a big change when you change cities, especially for a family," Pietrangelo said. "The Knights want to make life as easy as possible for our families and us so that we can worry about doing our job."

The Golden Knights' journey is often likened to that of a startup. The team was initially composed of players who were overlooked or deemed expendable by their former teams, earning them the moniker "Golden Misfits." Even today, this underdog spirit continues to define the team, with players like Amadio, Howden and Barbashev for his team's success.

The pursuit of talent also involved difficult choices. One such decision was to trade away defenseman Nate Schmidt to the Vancouver Canucks on October 12,

2020. This trade was made to accommodate the signing of Pietrangelo on the same day. Despite Schmidt's significant contributions to the team, the trade was executed without prior notice to him, illustrating the sometimes-abrupt nature of player transactions in professional sports.

Maintaining team chemistry was a concern for owner Bill Foley following Schmidt's departure. However, McPhee and McCrimmon were able to persuade Foley of the necessity of the move to clear cap space for Pietrangelo. This decision showcased the management's commitment to building a competitive roster.

The Knights had two great defensemen, Pietrangelo and Shea Theodore, with support from Zach Whitecloud. They had a tremendous two-way center in William Karlsson. Eichel gave them something they had never had before: a bona fide No. 1 center.

"One of the things our scouts really admired about Jack is his competitiveness. That's really been on display in the playoffs. Jack didn't have that opportunity in Buffalo along the way," McCrimmon said. "Jack was a young captain in Buffalo. Jack gets to be here in a room of really good leaders."

Original Misfit Brayden McNabb would add another trait to that list: ferocity.

"We were a ferocious team. We were playing fast, and it was hard on teams to keep up with us. And the belief set in," McNabb said.

Marchessault said that remains the Knights' mindset.

"The guys that have been here since day one, they're all resilient guys and they work hard," he said. "And I think that sets the tone, and everybody that comes there and kind of jumps on the same schedule as us."

The Dreaded Cap

Eichel, who commands the high salary of $10 million, represents one aspect of the Golden Knights' complex salary cap situation. Vegas has employed creative strategies to navigate the salary cap since the team's inception in 2017, including the trade of fan favorite Marc Andre Fleury. These maneuvers were executed strategically and contributed to the team's ability to win the Stanley Cup.

The NHL's salary cap serves two primary purposes: limiting player compensation and providing team executives with opportunities to work within the established cap system to maximize their rosters at different times of the season. It's a balance that teams must strike, and the Golden Knights have done so effectively.

According to Cap Friendly, the Golden Knights had a total cap hit of nearly $96.5 million, which exceeded the NHL's salary cap of $82.5 million for the season. They managed this overage by utilizing long-term injured reserve (LTIR), where they stashed nearly $13 off their total cap hit. This approach allowed them to remain competitive while staying within the league's rules.

Some of that LTIR money comes from Lehner. The Knights announced on Aug. 11, 2022, that Lehner would miss the entire season due to hip surgery. The free agent frenzy had waned. The Knights didn't have the cap space to scramble for a starter as the Colorado Avalanche had the year before in acquiring Darcy Kuemper after Philipp Grubauer left for Seattle.

Vegas has manipulated the system since it added its first player in 2017, and it worked the rules to win a Stanley Cup.

Egos In Check

Cassidy acknowledged that managing egos within the team has been essential, especially considering the star power on the Golden Knights' roster. While the players are individually talented and carry their own recognition, they have found a way to work together effectively.

"We're the guys that weren't wanted," Coach Cassidy said, himself fired by the Bruins weeks before the Knights hired him in the summer of 2022.

Cassidy points to players such as Amadio, a waiver pickup from Toronto, and Brett Howden, acquired via trade from the Rangers, and role player Chandler Stevenson.

"They're not walking into a room and saying, 'Geez, these guys were drafted and developed here and I'm an outsider.' They walk into a room where Marchessault and Reilly Smith and other guys have been through this," he said. "So, they have that togetherness or bond of maybe not being wanted the first time around by their teams."

The addition of the shot-blocking master in Alec Martinez also was critical, particularly in the Finals. Martinez won a Cup with the Kings, and his steady presence was felt in the locker room.

"Ever since I was traded here, we had a lot of really good players and a lot of really good guys. And this year, we have a couple characters in the locker room that have been added. That certainly adds that camaraderie side of it," Martinez said. "I know it's cliché, but we genuinely really enjoy hanging out with each other. And I've never been a part of a successful team that hasn't been that way. If you don't have that feeling off the ice, then it's going to carry over, and you're not going to have that feeling on the ice. So, I genuinely think the guys really love each other."

To hear the players tell it, it's an optimum place to work.

"It's fun to come to the office every day. We enjoy it. Even when things aren't going well, we still enjoy each other as people, which is a good thing," Pietrangelo said. "There are days when you don't want to go out (on the ice). But when you keep the energy up with each other, that kind of keeps it going."

Cassidy believes that chemistry starts in Summerlin, a planned community located northwest of Las Vegas, and has become a focal point for the team.

Foley invested in the construction of a state-of-the-art practice facility there, and many team members call the area home. This sense of community contributes to the team's success. Located just outside the Vegas city limits, with the Red Rock Canyon to the west, Summerlin is a planned community where Foley built the team's world-class practice facility where many players have short travel times to get thre.

"One thing I've learned in Vegas is that everyone lives in Summerlin, which is about 25 minutes away. The bonding is happening a little because everyone's in the same community," Cassidy said. "The guys are sharing rides. The wives are together, you know what I mean? It's not like a big city where everyone's going in a different direction as soon as practice is over. It's a little bit unique, maybe compared to some other markets. I think that's helped. I think the guys just genuinely like each other. You don't always get that. We have it. And most of the good teams find a way to have it."

William Carrier said a lot of that success has to do with how the teams are constructed.

"I think since Day 1, they built the team to have guys that play the right role, right? There are no skill guys on the fourth line trying to push up," he said. "It's a credit to them, building teams year after year."

Colin Miller, an original Golden Knight who saw them defeat his Dallas Stars in the Western Conference finals this year, was once part of that depth. He said Vegas was good at identifying players in other organizations and giving them the chance to excel.

"Sometimes these guys are great players, but they just don't get the opportunity elsewhere," he said.

Foley Only Needed Six

The Vegas Golden Knights have gone from an expansion franchise to Stanley Cup champions in just six seasons of existence. When Foley first announced he had won the rights to the team, he predicted a Cup in seven years, then amended that. Vegas hoisted the Stanley Cup following a convincing 9-3 win over the Florida Panthers in Game 5.

"Stanley Cup in six, that's the standard," Foley said shortly after securing the franchise.

Their postseason glory was quite impressive, but it was a long road to get there. It was one that was filled with some initial success combined with tinkering with an already talented roster.

It's fair to say that a Stanley Cup wouldn't have been possible without the selection of star winger Marchessault. Ironically enough, the Golden Knights selected the 2023 Conn Smythe winner from the Panthers on draft night. Marchessault was coming off a season in which he registered 51 points (30 goals and 21 assists), but Florida chose not to protect him during the Expansion Draft process, a move they deeply regret.

The Golden Knights also hit a home run with two of their defensemen, Theodore and McNabb. Theodore was acquired from the Anaheim Ducks in exchange for defenseman Clayton Stoner. Theodore ended up tallying a goal and five assists in the Stanley Cup Final, while McNabb added a pair of assists.

Acquisitions of Eichel and Stone were critical, but all the Knights contriibuted during the season and the playoffs. With the early success, the Golden Knights made a huge splash at the 2019 trade deadline when the team acquired star winger Stone in exchange for defenseman Erik Brannstrom, center Oscar Lindberg and a 2020 second-round pick. Stone quickly planted his roots in Vegas as he signed an eight-year, $76 million contract extension with the franchise.

Injuries became a common theme for Stone throughout his Golden Knights tenure. He's played 55 games or less in each of the last three regular seasons, including only playing in 43 games during the 2022-23 season due to a back injury. Despite not playing since Jan. 12, Stone returned for the start of the team's playoff run against the Winnipeg Jets.

He proved to be a force as he compiled 24 points (11 goals and 13 assists), which was the third highest among Vegas players. When the Golden Knights needed him the most, Stone recorded a hat trick in Game 5 of the Stanley Cup Final and became the first NHL player since Colorado Avalanche star Peter Forsberg in 1996 to have a hat trick in a Stanley Cup Final game.

Stone and Eichel brought star power and crucial playoff performances to the Golden Knights, adding depth and skill to an already talented roster. Their contributions and those of other key players helped Vegas secure their first Stanley Cup, a rare early feat for an expansion team.

The 2022-23 season was much kinder to Eichel and the rest of the Golden Knights. Eichel racked up 66 27 goals and 39 assists, which was the third-highest point total of his career. The 26-year-old even returned to Buffalo and registered a hat trick against his former team. Eichel did miss some time with a lower-body injury, but he really turned it on come playoff time. Eichel ended up leading the Golden Knights with 25 points (six goals and 20 assists) during the Stanley Cup Playoffs. He had a sensational postseason that included becoming a more dynamic two-way player in Coach Bruce Cassidy's system. While Marchessault took home Conn Smythe honors, there's no way the Golden Knights take home the Cup without Eichel's stickhandling ability.

Goalie Shuffle

Late in the 2022 offseason, Vegas was dealt a brutal blow when the team learned that goaltender Robin Lehner would have to undergo hip surgery and miss the entire 2022-23 season. During the season, the team acquired netminder Hill from the San Jose Sharks for a 2024 fourth-round pick.

The Golden Knights entered the 2022-23 season with Logan Thompson as the team's starting goalie, and that proved to be a great decision. Thompson had a strong first half and even was selected to his first career All-Star Game. However, Thompson dealt with a lower-body injury down the stretch and didn't play in the postseason.

Hill thrived throughout the Stanley Cup Final as he posted a 2.40 goals-against-average and won four of his five starts. Hill also made arguably the most impressive save of the postseason when he stopped Nick Cousins with his goalie stick at point-blank range. His miraculous saves early in games kept Florida off the scoreboard.

Difference Makers

Who wouldn't want one of the league's best shot blockers with two Stanley Cup titles to his credit? Not the L.A. Kings. Defenseman Alec Martinez joined the Knights in the 2019-20 season, back when there was still a "Fun Committee." He won two Stanley Cups with the Kings and helped Vegas reach the playoffs two times before breaking through this season.

During the playoffs, as well as the regular season, Martinez is a shot-blocking machine.

Cassidy puts Vegas Over the Top

For an NHL franchise that only existed for five seasons, the Golden Knights already were on their third head coach. Gerard Gallant was originally at the helm in 2017 and did have great success throughout his tenure. Gallant produced a 118-75-20 record (256 points) and won the Jack Adams Award as the league's best head coach in the 2017-18 campaign. Still, the veteran

bench boss ended up being fired midway through the 2019-20 season.

The Golden Knights hired Peter DeBoer for the next two seasons, and DeBoer was also quite successful. DeBoer tallied a 98-50-12 record (208 points), but Vegas missed the postseason for the first time in franchise history during the 2021-22 season. After missing the Stanley Cup Playoffs, DeBoer was canned.

Enter Cassidy. Cassidy was relieved of his duties with the Boston Bruins despite taking the team to the Stanley Cup Playoffs in each of his six seasons in Boston. The 58-year-old certainly didn't last on the market long. In fact, the Golden Knights hired Cassidy as the team's head coach just eight days after he was shown the door by the Bruins. After falling just short of winning the 2019 Stanley Cup Finals as the Bruins coach, Cassidy got the job done this time around with a very talented roster.

In Cassidy, Vegas finally found the voice that they had been searching for since the franchise was founded. In his first season with the Golden Knights, Cassidy helped lead the team to a 51-22-9 record and a franchise-best 111 points. Cassidy placed more importance on defense, and the Golden Knights clearly bought into it quickly. Defenseman Martinez blocked 244 shots to lead the league in that category, while teammate McNabb had the second-most blocks (197). In addition, fellow blue-liner Pietrangelo finished with the seventh-most blocked shots (177). Jack Eichel also established himself as more of a two-way player under Cassidy's reign.

Tough Decisions are Rewarded

During the pursuit of a championship, there are often tough decisions that need to be made, and the Golden Knights made a few big ones in recent years.

For his performance during the 2020-21 season, goaltender Marc-Andre Fleury produced a spectacular 1.98 goals-against-average and won the Vezina Trophy as the league's top goalie.

However, just one month after winning the prestigious award, Fleury was traded to the Chicago Blackhawks because the Golden Knights needed to clear salary cap space. It marked the first time the Vezina Trophy winner was traded since Dominik Hasek was moved back in 2001.

In the 2022 offseason, still needing to clear salary cap space, Vegas traded star forward Max Pacioretty to the Carolina Hurricanes. The Golden Knights acquired Pacioretty to be an integral part of the team in 2018, but they simply had to make a move. Vegas was forced to rely on role players, such as Brett Howden and Nicolas Roy, to help fill the void left by Pacioretty.

The Locker Room Vibe

Foley had an edict for his management team: Find players who were "team effort, low ego, low maintenance."

Marchessault said ferocity remains the Knights' mindset.

"The guys that have been here since day one, they're all resilient guys and they work hard," he said. "And I think that sets the tone, and everybody that comes there and kind of jumps on the same schedule as us."

Day 1 is the first day on the job for every employee. Those original Knights – cast aside by their teams for various reasons and dubbed the "Golden Misfits" – all landed on the same roster together at the same time.

It's not an audacious startup anymore but rather a sustained healthy environment.

Vegas has been solid since its inception. The Knights have the sixth best regular-season points percentage (.632) and the second-most playoff wins (53) of any team since entering the NHL.

Colin Miller, an original Golden Knight who saw them defeat his Dallas Stars in the Western Conference finals in 2023, was once part of that depth. He said Vegas was good at identifying players in other organizations and giving them the chance to excel.

"Sometimes these guys are great players, but they just don't get the opportunity elsewhere," he said.

Cassidy said that the egos in the room have been held in check but that the magnitude of the star power on the roster isn't ignored. "It's about the crest on the front, not the name on the back, and you can still have respect for what they've accomplished. So, there's always that balance," he said.

All these factors are crucial in winning a title. After Foley originally stated he needed seven years to bring Las Vegas a title, he had to revise his promise.

The quest for a dynasty began again in 2023-2024.

Vegas Golden Knights

Conference: NHL Western
Division: Pacific
Founded: 2017
History: Vegas Golden Knights 2017-present

Home arena: T-Mobile Arena
Location: Paradise, Nevada
Owners: Black Knight Sports and Entertainment (Bill Foley) (70%) Maloof family (30%)

GM: Kelly McCrimmon
Head Coach   Bruce Cassidy
Captain   Mark Stone

Minor league affiliates:
Henderson Silver Knights (AHL)
Savannah Ghost Pirates (ECHL)

Stanley Cups 1 (2022-2023)
Conference championships (2)
    (2017-2018, 2022-2023
Division championships (3)
    (2017-2018, 2019-2020, 2022-2023)
Official website: nhl.com/goldenknights

Chapter 15
HAIL, THE GOLDEN KNIGHTS!

The Golden Knights routed the Florida Panthers 9-3 to capture the franchise's first NHL championship. The Panthers had pulled off upset after upset to reach the Final, but fell to the deep Golden Knights, who went efficiently through the playoffs, winning their title in 22 games.

Captain Mark Stone scored a hat trick, the first in a Stanley Cup Final since the Colorado Avalanche's Peter Forsberg scored three in a 1996 game, and the Golden Knights pulled away in a dominant second period. That allowed Vegas to celebrate on home ice a little more than five years after the Washington Capitals had clinched the 2018 title at Las Vegas' T-Mobile Arena.

"Unbelievable," Stone said. "The look in my teammates' eyes when I got (the Stanley Cup), one of the craziest feelings I've ever had. I can't even describe the feelings in my stomach right now. It's everything you can imagine."

A closer look at Game 5:

Coach Bruce Cassidy also put out five of the six original players in the starting lineup.The Panthers' power play had struggled throughout the Final and it put them behind in Game 5.

Vegas goalie Adin Hill stopped Aleksander Barkov in close and soon after, Stone took advantage of a turnover to start a 2-on-1 break with Chandler Stephenson. With the pass taken away, he made a slick move in front of the net and shot the puck past Panthers goalie Sergei Bobrovsky for a short-handed goal. The Golden Knights took advantage of another odd-man break less than two minutes later, and defenseman Nicolas Hague finished it off by firing a loose puck into the net.

In the second period, Florida defenseman Aaron Ekblad cut the deficit to 2-1 with a shot through a screen, then Vegas took over again. Defenseman Alec Martinez put Vegas back up by two goals nine years after he had scored the Cup-clinching goal for the Los Angeles Kings in 2014.

Shea Theodore and William Karlsson set up fellow original Golden Knight Reilly Smith to make it 4-1 before Stone made it 5-1 on a one-timer. Michael Amadio finished up the dominant period, putting his own rebound past Bobrovsky with 1.2 seconds left. Vegas' Ivan Barbashev made it 7-1 in the third period before Florida's Sam Reinhart and Sam Bennett scored. Stone's third goal was scored into an empty net at 14:06 and Nicolas Roy scored the final goal with just over a minute to play.

Even though the game was a rout, Hill had to come up with big saves. He stopped Anton Lundell early, made the save on Barkov and robbed Anthony Duclair with a glove save in the third period. Hill was one of five goalies that the Golden Knights used during the regular season. He entered play after Laurent Brossoit was injured in the second round and went 11-4 the rest of the playoffs.

Marchessault, who was left unprotected by the Panthers in the expansion draft, won the award for playoff MVP. He finished with 13 goals, tied for the playoff lead, and 25 points, which was second overall.

"He went on a heck of a run," said Eichel, who led playoff scoring in his first postseason appearance. "So deserving of the Conn Smythe. I'm so happy for him. He's been here since the beginning."

Stone, as is tradition for the team captain, got to lift the Stanley Cup first. He handed off to Smith and the remaining original members of the Knights got their turn.

The Champions dominated the Finals and here's the road taken to the top. The Boston Bruins won the Presidents' Trophy for the best record in the league and entered the playoffs after setting NHL records for wins (64) and points (135), but couldn't make it out of the first round with as the Florida Panthers pulled an upset in Game 7.

In the West, the Colorado Avalanche was the top seed, but the Avalanche couldn't defend their title. The Vegas Golden Knights qualified for the playoffs on the final day of the regular season and battled their way to NHL immortality.

Road To The Cup

STRANLEY CUP FINALS
(1) Vegas Golden Knights vs. Florida Panthers VGK wins, 4-1
Game 1: Golden Knights 5, Panthers 2
Game 2: Golden Knights 7, Panthers
Game 3: Panthers 3, Golden Knights 2 (OT)
Game 4: Golden Knights 3, Panthers 2
Game 5: Golden Knights 9, Panthers 3
Conference finals results

EASTERN CONFERENCE
(1) Carolina Hurricanes vs. Florida Panthers FLA wins, 4-0
Game1: Panthers 3, Hurricanes 2 (4OT)
Game2: Panthers 2, Hurricanes 1 (OT)
Game 3: Panthers 1, Hurricanes 0
Game 4: Panthers 4, Hurricanes 3

WESTERN CONFERENCE
(1) Vegas Golden Knights vs. (2) Dallas Stars VGK wins, 4-2
Game 1: Golden Knights 4, Stars 3 (OT)
Game 2: Golden Knights 3, Stars 2 (OT)
Game 3: Golden Knights 4, Stars 0
Game 4: Stars 3, Golden Knights 2 (OT)
Game 5: Stars 4, Golden Knights 2
Game 6: Golden Knights 6, Stars 0

Second round results
EASTERN CONFERENCE
(2) Maple Leafs vs. (WC2) Florida Panthers FLA wins, 4-1
Game 1: Panthers 4, Maple Leafs 2
Game 2: Panthers 3, Maple Leafs 2
Game 3: Panthers 3, Maple Leafs 2 (OT)
Game 4: Maple Leafs 2, Panthers 1
Game 5: Panthers 3, Maple Leafs 2 (OT)
Carolina Hurricanes vs. (2) New Jersey Devils CAR wins, 4-1
Game 1: Hurricanes 5, Devils 1
Game 2: Hurricanes 6, Devils 1
Game 3: Devils 8, Hurricanes 4
Game 4: Hurricanes 6, Devils 1
Game 5: Hurricanes 3, Devils 2 (OT) I

WESTERN CONFERENCE
Vegas Golden Knights vs. (2) Edmonton Oilers VGK wins, 4-2
Game 1: Golden Knights 5, Oilers 4
Game 2: Oilers 5, Golden Knights 1
Game 3: Golden Knights 5, Oilers 1
Game 4: Oilers 4, Golden Knights 1
Game 4: Golden Knights 4, Oilers 3
Game 6: Golden Knights 5, Oilers 2

(2) Dallas Stars vs. (WC1) Seattle Kraken DAL wins, 4-3
Game 1: Kraken 5, Stars 4 (OT)
Game 2: Stars 4, Kraken 2
Game 3: Kraken 7, Stars 2
Game 4: Stars 6, Kraken 3
Game 5: Stars 5, Kraken 2
Game 6: Kraken 6, Stars 3
Game 7: Stars 2, Kraken 1
First round results
EASTERN CONFERENCE
(WC2) Florida Panthers vs. Boston Bruins FLA wins, 4-3

Game 1: Bruins 3, Panthers 1
Game 2: Panthers 6, Bruins 3
Game 3: Bruins 4, Panthers 2
Game 4: Bruins 6, Panthers 2
Game 5: Panthers 4, Bruins 3 (OT)
Game 6: Panthers 7, Bruins 5
Game 7: Panthers 4, Bruins 3

(2) Maple Leafs vs. (3) Tampa Bay Lightning TOR wins, 4-2
Game 1:Lightning 7, Maple Leafs 3
Game 2:Maple Leafs 7, Lightning 2
Game 3:Maple Leafs 4, Lightning 3 (OT)
Game 4:Maple Leafs 5, Lightning 4 (OT)
Game 5:Lightning 4, Maple Leafs 2
Game 6:Maple Leafs 2, Lightning 1 (OT)

(1) Carolina Hurricanes vs. New York Islanders CAR wins, 4-2
Game 1:Hurricanes 2, Islanders 1
Game 2:Hurricanes 4, Islanders 3 (OT)
Game 3:Islanders 5, Hurricanes 1
Game 4:Hurricanes 5, Islanders 2
Game 5:Islanders 3, Hurricanes 2
Game 6:Hurricanes 2, Islanders 1 (OT)

2) New Jersey Devils vs. New York Rangers NJ wins, 4-3
Game 1:Rangers 5, Devils 1
Game 2:Rangers 5, Devils 1
Game 3:Devils 2, Rangers 1 (OT) |
Game 4:Devils 3, Rangers 1
Game 5:Devils 4, Rangers 0
Game 6:Rangers 5, Devils 2
Game 7:Devils 4, Rangers 0

WESTERN CONFERENCE
(1) Golden Knights vs. (WC2) Winnipeg Jets VGK wins, 4-1
Game 1:Jets 5, Golden Knights 1
Game 2:Golden Knights 5, Jets 2
Game 3:Golden Knights 5, Jets 4 (2OT)
Game 4:Golden Knights 4, Jets 2
Game 5:Golden Knights 4, Jets 1
(2) Edmonton Oilers vs. (3) Los Angeles Kings EDM wins, 4-2
Game 1:Kings 4, Oilers 3 (OT)
Game 2:Oilers 4, Kings 2
Game 3:Kings 3, Oilers 2 (OT)
Game 4:Oilers 5, Kings 4 (OT)
Game 5:Oilers 6, Kings 3
Game 6:Oilers 5, Kings 4

(2) Dallas Stars vs. (3) Minnesota Wild DAL wins, 4-2
Game 1:Wild 3, Stars 2 (2OT)
Game 2:Stars 7, Wild 3
Game 3:Wild 5, Stars 1
Game 4:Stars 3, Wild 2
Game 5:Stars 4, Wild 0
Game 6:Stars 4, Wild 1
(WC1) Seattle Kraken vs. (1) Colorado Avalanche SEA wins, 4-3
Game 1: Kraken 3, Avalanche 1
Game 2: Avalanche 3, Kraken 2
Game 3: Avalanche 6, Kraken 4
Game 4: Kraken 3, Avalanche 2 (OT)
Game 5: Kraken 3, Avalanche 2
Game 6: Avalanche 4, Kraken 1
Game 7: Avalanche 2, Kraken 1

Author Biographies

Robert Lawson and his son, Blake.

Robert (Bob) Lawson III

Robert (Bob) Lawson III's journey is a study in versatility and commitment. With a life that spans multiple sectors, including sports, finance, manufacturing and now author, his myriad accomplishments are nothing short of extraordinary.

Sports Achievements: Motorcycle Racing: Lawson Associates, founded in 1989, marked Bob's entry into professional motorcycle racing. He showcased his managerial brilliance by handling top racers such as AMA Dirt Track Champion Jay Springsteen and World Superbike Champion Doug Polen. Bob's vision also led to the establishment of AMA Superbike/Super-Sport Teams – namely, American Eagle Racing and CNC Jobs Racing.

Ice Hockey in Las Vegas: Between 1993 and 1995, Bob redefined ice hockey in Las Vegas. As the General Manager, Marketing Director, and Director of Hockey Operations of Santa Fe Casino Ice Arena, Bob took the helm of the Las Vegas Aces Hockey Team. Under his leadership, the Aces garnered the distinction of being the first documented professional hockey team playing a full league schedule with exclusively paid players.

Las Vegas Aces: His passion for the sport was evident in his dual role as the GM and Head Coach of the Las Vegas Aces. For two seasons, Bob guided the team, imprinting his mark on every game.

Las Vegas Flash: Bob's impact on the Roller Hockey International (RHI) scene was significant. As the General Manager of the Las Vegas Flash, Bob's foresight brought "Miracle on Ice" Gold Medalist Ken Morrow onboard as the Head Coach.

Flint Generals Hockey Club: The 1995-1996 season was a golden era for the Flint Generals Hockey Club, much credited to Bob. Serving as the VP of Marketing, he was a core member of the management team, ensuring the club's first-ever championship year. Under Bob's watch, the club set records in sellout games and league sponsorships.

On the Golf Course: The greens and fairways were no stranger to try Club. He also showcased his talent as a touring professional across Florida and Georgia.

Business Ventures: CNC Jobs Inc.: Bob co-founded CNC Jobs Inc. in 2003, which, under his leadership as CEO, metamorphosed into a dominant entity in manufacturing and technology employment. Pioneering a video-supported job board with son Blake Lawson and partners Melissa Mohr-Lawson and Melissa Lawson, CNC Jobs Inc. stands as the top-rated employment source for manufacturing in the United States.

ThreadForms Inc.: A visionary at just 21, Bob, along with his mentor and father, Robert Lawson Jr., established ThreadForms Inc. This cutting tool company was a game-changer in the industry, revolutionizing shipment practices by delivering custom-designed tooling within 24 hours.

A Legacy Beyond Business: While Bob's professional achievements are commendable, his heart beats loudest for his family. His six grandchildren (Avah, Alexa, Dylan, Peyton, Jayden and Wesley) are a testament to his commitment to family values.

From the icy landscapes of Michigan to the high-stakes boardrooms, Bob Lawson's indomitable spirit has left an indelible mark. His legacy, built on adaptability, vision and an unyielding drive, will continue to inspire generations.

Dedication: "I have been blessed with an amazing life filled with many accomplishments and hardships. Special thanks to my son Blake, who has ridden my roller coaster life and career path and never left my side with his love, support, and, most of all, friendship. Additionally, to my wife Melissa (Missy) and the rest of my family and extended family, you have been there for whatever my crazy life has been.

But most of all, to God for always opening that door for me when another slammed shut."

Richard Gubbe

Richard Gubbe and his daughter, Rachel Gubbe.

Richard Gubbe has had a multi-faceted career that has encompassed writing, public relations and event production. He's held the positions of lead writer for Caesars Palace, editor-in-chief and lead writer for Las Vegas Magazine and features editor and magazine editor for the Las Vegas SUN. He's won writing awards for the Rock River Times, as a contributing writer for Elevate Magazine and as Sports Editor for Tazewell Publishing's stable of five newspapers on Illinois. He has freelance credits with USA Today, The Sporting News and Singapore Women's Weekly, Showbiz magazine, Nevadan magazine and Nevada Woman magazine. Whether it's investigative reporting, feature writing, editorial writing or business writing, he has excelled on all platforms, and he's interviewed some of the biggest names in show business and sports.

Gubbe was responsible for creating a casino customer magazine for Caesars, as well as the formation of a video library that catalogued movies, television shows and events held on the property. He also has been a public relations and sports marketing specialist for various entities in Nevada and Illinois.

Gubbe has helped produce some of the largest events in Las Vegas sports, including the lead coordinator for the outdoor hockey game at Caesars, the first ever pro hockey event in Las Vegas. His ice hockey career included playing in leagues in Illinois and Las Vegas that included a tryout with the New York Rangers in 1983. Other special events he helped promote include the lead coordinator for the Robbie Knievel Jump Over the Fountains at Caesars, worldwide boxing and kickboxing at Caesars, the Miss Universe Pageant, as well as off-road racing and hydroplane races in Nevada and Hawaii. He holds the attendance record for many events, including the Kickboxing Extravaganza for Showtime at the T&M in Las Vegas.

Gubbe won Illinois Press Association awards for his 23-part, award-winning series on toxic waste dumping in Northern Illinois – for Investigative Reporting (First Place) and another for News Reporting (Second Place). He won two consecutive first-place awards for Explanatory Journalism from the Nevada Press Association and writing and section awards for Tazewell Publishing.

Other positions held include copy editor for the Green Bay Press-Gazette, copy editor for the Southern Illinoisan and copy editor for Rockford Newspapers – serving in the areas of news, sports, features, health, business, travel and food that included page design work.

Along with writing news and feature stories and coordinating events at Caesars Palace, Gubbe performed event production for Image Media and PR for the Las Vegas Aces, Las Vegas Flash and he served as an event consultant for the United States Navy. His PR writing and event credits are too numerous to mention.

Gubbe initiated a newspaper at Clark County Community College (College of Southern Nevada) while serving as an instructor, and he taught writing classes for continuing education programs. He also has been a ghost writer for two books and has been a grant writer for numerous charities in Nevada and Northern Illinois.

He's also had a 35-year career as a Reiki Master Teacher in Illinois and Nevada with more than 3,000 students in his classes. He taught at Clark County Community College in Las Vegas, and at Rock Valley College and Swedish American Hospital in Rockford, Ill. He served as president of Reiki Energy International, a nonprofit group.

He received his bachelor's degree in journalism in 1977 from Southern Illinois University, serving as a paid staff writer for the 25,000 circulation Daily Egyptian student newspaper.

"My gratifying career has been filled with high-profile stories, celebrity interviews and record attendance for many events," Gubbe says. "My hard work has resulted in accolades, successes and unforgettable memories. I made the best of every opportunity."

Dedication: "I would like to thank my family for their unwavering support while battling a horrendous genetic lung disease and being born legally blind – siblings Peter Gubbe, Mary Lee and Barbara Edmunds; brother-in-law Bob Edmunds; my daughter, Rachel Lynne Gubbe and fiancé Adam Collier; my stepson, Aaron LeQuire, and Jewel Foster; and Rachel and Aaron's mother, Lynn. They have brought immeasurable love and joy to my life."